LIFE IS JUST A RIDE!

A map to help you remember the
truth that is already inside you

Jocelyne Grzela, CHt

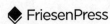 FriesenPress

Suite 300 - 990 Fort St
Victoria, BC, v8v 3K2
Canada

www.friesenpress.com

ISBN
978-1-5255-9782-4 (Hardcover)
978-1-5255-9781-7 (Paperback)
978-1-5255-9783-1 (eBook)

1. BODY, MIND & SPIRIT, INSPIRATION & PERSONAL GROWTH

Distributed to the trade by The Ingram Book Company

CONTENTS

INTRODUCTION

If you're reading this book, you are most likely ready to hear the messages in these pages at this moment of your journey. This book is not about trying to convince you of anything and not about telling you what to do. It is meant to inspire you to find your own truth. It is my hope that you realize that you have a choice to live in fear or live free as you were meant to be. If the information you find here inspires you and works for you, apply it in your life. What I am sharing with you here are my personal experiences. There are many paths up the mountain. Mine is not a better way or the only way; it is just a way that has helped me make sense of the great challenges of loss, divorce, trauma, and a brush with death.

When we arrive in this world, many tools are made available to us to guide us as we set out on our journey. Once we find these tools and use them to connect the pieces, we begin to create a map to help us understand who we are and what we're doing here. We are provided with what we need to begin enjoying the game we have chosen to partake in. In this book, I will share with you some of the tools I have personally found useful on my path, tools I have also shared in my workshops and with clients in my private hypnotherapy practice. This information will help you create your own treasure map to help you remember who you are.

Applying the knowledge and wisdom of my life experiences has helped me see through the illusion to remember who I really am. I hope these insights will do the same for you. I don't know how soon you will begin to notice changes in your life, but I do know that you will be pleasantly surprised to have it happen at just the right time for you. Use what resonates with you and discard what doesn't. What resonates is a confirmation that this knowledge is already within you, and this may just be a gentle awakening. Keep an open mind. Be open to thinking outside the box, perhaps even throwing the box away. You must unlearn what you have learned. For now, set aside your previous beliefs and allow for new possibilities. Don't go searching for another set of beliefs; seek to remember the truth that is already inside you.

I have always picked up at least one gem of wisdom from every book I have read. Maybe you will have an ah-ha moment as you read these pages as I did when I first read the following:

> "Believe nothing, no matter where you read it or who has said it, not even if I have said it, unless it agrees with your own reason and your own common sense."[1] — Buddha

---

1 https://www.goodreads.com/author/quotes/5805904.Budha

CHAPTER 1

DESTINED TO BE A TEACHER

In a small town in a remote area of Northern Ontario, Canada, there weren't many career options available in the mid-seventies. You had the choice of becoming a nurse, a teacher, or a secretary. If there were other options, we weren't made aware of them. Nursing was absolutely out of the question for me. I had no interest in that whatsoever, and since I come from a family of teachers, that seemed to be the obvious choice for me as well. I followed in the footsteps of my older sisters. Even my mother had been a schoolteacher when she was just a teenager in the 1930s. There were no high schools nearby in those years, so once she had reached the highest available elementary school year, she started teaching the younger children who were just coming in. One of my favorite activities as a child was to play the role of the teacher, and my students were my nieces and nephews. I was a dedicated student throughout all my school years, and I even skipped a few grades, which meant that I entered university at a very young age. I made the obvious choice of becoming a teacher, and my first career as an elementary schoolteacher began when I was just eighteen years old.

Being the youngest of thirteen children and being the youngest among classmates, from having skipped a few grades, I had a severe lack of self-confidence. You would think that since I was usually at the top of my classes, I would be a leader, ready to take on the world, but it was quite the opposite. I believed that because everyone was older and bigger than me, they must also be smarter. So, I was very shy and introverted, and the fact that I didn't speak a word of English did not help the situation at all. My eighth-grade teacher reminded me of that often, as he would make fun of me in front of the class when he tried to teach us English.

When I met the man who was to become my first husband, I was in my last year of high school. He was thirteen years older than me, but we fell in love. I knew I had to be with him. When I left to go to university, he followed, and we moved in together. We got married less than a year later. My mother was strongly against me living with and marrying an older man, and she refused to accept him. He was not welcome in her house. According to her beliefs and opinion, he was not a good man and was much too old for me. Her judgments added another level of anxiety that I had not anticipated. "If she would only take the time to get to know him," I thought, "she would see that he is a good person, with a good heart, who cares about me and loves me." Even though I was only nineteen, I was more mature than most at that age, and this relationship felt right to me. I was aware of the age difference, but age is just a number, and I really wanted to point out to my mother that she had married a man who was eleven years older than she was, but I didn't. It was hard for me to understand her reasoning. As long as he wasn't welcome in her home, I refused to give in and didn't go visit either. This situation continued for five years until she finally opened up and accepted him with open arms.

Fresh out of university, I was hired as a French Immersion teacher and found myself in front of a classroom full of rambunctious eight-year-olds, who didn't understand a word I said since this was, after all, French Immersion, and they spoke only English. Within that first week of school, I broke out in hives! What had I gotten myself into? All my insecurities showed up to the party, and I began to wonder if I was smart enough to do this. The parents spoke only English, so how was I going to communicate with them on how their children were doing? Parent-teacher interviews were kind of interesting. With the help of my husband, teaching me how to speak English and helping me write report cards, I made it through my first year of teaching. Everything improved immensely the following years, the children and their parents loved me, and I became fluent in English.

The time spent in the classroom with the students was enjoyable, but since this was a brand-new program being offered in schools, the school board required much testing to be done. That meant that many days were spent testing the children's progress and having an audience of parents and school board members at the back of the room, observing my every move. Not stressful at all! I just wanted to be left alone to teach, but being constantly under a magnifying glass turned an enjoyable experience into an unpleasant situation. After six years of teaching, I was burned out. Being under that much pressure every day was exhausting. I knew I didn't want to do that for the rest of my life, but I didn't know what I wanted to do.

All Is Well on My Spiritual Journey

Even though I am a teacher at heart, I learned early on that teaching isn't confined to the classroom. So, I left my short teaching career in search of something more. I've always loved helping people, which is one of the reasons for writing this book.

From a young age, I wondered about the mysteries of life and the universe. I knew there had to be so much more, and my focus veered toward self-development and self-improvement, always searching for answers. Reading has always been high on my list of priorities, and the first book that literally fell off the shelf, landing at my feet, was *The Power of Your Subconscious Mind* by Joseph Murphy. That was the start of my true soul-seeking journey. I was hooked. I knew I was more than just my conscious mind, and I wanted to dig deeper.

I quickly realized the importance of meditation as a way to access deeper levels of the mind, and I started meditating every morning. I was twenty-six years old.

Having married a man with a sense of adventure, who was always seeking greener grass on the other side of the fence, we moved often, not just across town, but to different towns and eventually, to another country. After several years of trying out a few different jobs, and then replacing those efforts with self-employment, we decided it was time for a monumental change. We were both tired of living in a cold climate, so, in 1989, we sold our house and moved from Canada to the United States. We wanted to go as far south as we could, while remaining in North America.

They say we help each other grow in relationships, and my husband had many qualities I admired. He was definitely instrumental in getting me out of my shell, and before long, I shared his sense of adventure. Although at times, he decided, and I just went along because he was older, and I thought he knew better.

This move was extremely high on the scale of new and exciting adventures. It overshadowed the fact that I was leaving my family behind and moving to another country. Wow, we were moving to the Sunshine State!

We had traded the long, cold winters of Canada for the sunshine and the warmth of Florida. The further south we drove, the more exhilarating the experience became. I will always remember that moment on Interstate 75 when we crossed the Georgia state line into Florida. There it was: Welcome to FLORIDA, THE SUNSHINE STATE. In front of us, there was only blue sky, sunshine, and palm trees. With the windows rolled down, we could feel the warmth, and we could smell the salty air of the ocean. This was beyond our wildest dream. How lucky were we to have been able to make this happen? No more cold winters, no more snow! Total contentment.

We were able to move to Florida because my husband had obtained a work visa through the Free Trade Agreement between Canada and the United States. Life in this new chapter was amazing in the beginning. We used a large portion of the money from the sale of our house in Toronto as a down payment on a house in Florida, and we would have enough money to live on until the paychecks started coming in. Since my husband was promised a substantial salary from his new employer, he insisted on keeping up with the lifestyle we had been accustomed to in Canada. We needed a beautiful house with a pool, an expensive car, and, of course, we also had to get a boat right away. All that was great. We were living in paradise, but I was really worried about our finances. Of all the qualities my husband had, saving money was not one of them. He was never good at saving for a rainy day. If there was money in the account, it had to be spent, and I mean, all of it, to the last penny. That was one area we definitely did not agree on.

After several months, he realized that his salary was nowhere near what he had been promised. Our bank account was empty, and I was not able to work until we had been in the country for five years and could obtain a green card. We struggled for the next four years until I was able to start working and get us back on track.

There was a silver lining in all of this, and there always is. The five years I spent at home were not wasted, as they gave me the ideal opportunity to focus on my personal development. This period allowed me plenty of time every day to focus on meditation, which led me even deeper on my spiritual path. I found a job that I really enjoyed all while pursuing my passion for spiritual growth. My circle of friends was expanding, and I was led to join an Edgar Cayce study group. Edgar Cayce, known as the sleeping prophet, was an American clairvoyant who channeled information on subjects such as reincarnation, dreams, healing, and future events while in a self-induced sleep state. I had read several books about this man and saw this as a great opportunity. This study group was exactly what I needed and where I needed to be. I had found my tribe, a group of like-minded people who shared my passion. The natural teacher in me wanted to share what I knew. I had been a very successful meditator, and, shortly after joining the group, I offered to guide them in meditation. After that first night, everyone agreed that I should lead all the group meditations from then on. "You're a natural," they said. "I've never experienced such deep levels of relaxation." For many years after that, I also led group meditations for hundreds of people who attended our annual retreats, and I was always asked if I was a certified meditation teacher or therapist. I was truly flying. This experience was exactly what I had visualized during my daily meditations years before. After a few years of leading the group meditation at the annual retreats, one of our guest speakers at the retreat just happened to be a hypnotherapist, who taught at the Association for Research and Enlightenment in Virginia Beach, Virginia. It was happening. I had the answer. Everything was so clear; I finally knew what I wanted to do with my life. I had found my purpose! I was ready to learn, and the right teacher had just appeared.

So, in my early forties, I went back to school and became a certified hypnotherapist and past-life regression therapist at the Association for Research and Enlightenment. I accomplished a meaningful goal, something I had dreamed of doing for many years, and I opened a private practice immediately after graduating. In addition, I began teaching monthly workshops and group meditations. In my opinion, the best way to learn something thoroughly is to teach it. That was true for me. Those were truly magnificent and magical years. I was living my life's purpose of helping people overcome whatever was preventing them from achieving their highest potential, and for some, my goal was to alleviate their pain and suffering. Life was wonderful. I was living my passion, but, apparently, the universe had a different plan for me.

Never thought I'd find myself in such a place in my early fifties. Just when you think you have your life and future all figured out, it can all disappear, and you find yourself saying, "what just happened?"

CHAPTER 2

WHAT JUST HAPPENED?
LIFE TAKES A MAJOR DETOUR

The deeper I went into my inner search for life's meaning, the more I realized I was not as happy as I pretended to be on the surface. I was happy with my spiritual growth, passionate about my hypnotherapy practice, and teaching meditation classes. I was finally living my life's purpose of being, doing, and teaching what I love, but I was very unhappy in my marriage. The drifting apart was becoming undeniable. Life had remained the same for my husband; there didn't appear to be any more growth on his part, while I was very driven and determined to follow my path. He was emotionally absent. No matter how much I tried to communicate, he ignored me. It was impossible to have a conversation that lasted more than two minutes, his attention would drift elsewhere. As much as we had in common for many years, we were now on completely different highways and no longer shared the same passions. I knew I could not continue living this way; I was miserable.

Looking back at the early years of our marriage, I realized that I had put up with many selfish behaviors that I could no longer tolerate twenty years later. The moment that sealed the deal for me was the time my father passed away. My husband and I flew up to our hometown for the funeral, and I experienced the worst week of my life. No one is ever really prepared when we lose someone we love. I thought I was, since my understanding of death was that it is just a transition. Everything is energy and energy never dies; it's just transformed. So, we don't really die, we just leave the physical vehicle behind, and we're still connected at a deeper level of consciousness. I had read many books; I had experienced and taught past-life regressions, and there seemed to be reliable information and evidence of the soul continuing on. Even though I knew all that, when my father died, I lost it. All that wisdom had been replaced with a deep, uncontrollable sadness. The little girl inside me, who had just lost her father, came back and was overwhelmed with grief. My husband became angry with me for spending so much time with my brothers and sisters while we were at the funeral home. He felt ignored, but in my mind, that seemed ridiculous. I believe it is quite normal for siblings, who have just lost a parent, to come together at a time like this, especially as people came to pay their respects to a man that they had all loved.

On the flight back from northern Canada to Florida, I received the silent treatment. Oh, yes, that had become his way of reacting when something didn't go his way. Being on such an emotional roller coaster during that week had left my immune system drained and, therefore, susceptible to catching a cold. I felt terrible. It was a long, miserable flight. When we were finally home, he was furious at me for the way I had fallen apart, and he told me that I should have known better with all the spiritual awareness I had achieved. After a week of constant criticism, I had enough. This was not a healthy environment.

In my mid-forties, I decided to end my marriage of twenty-six years. This, however, did not happen overnight. I had been contemplating and meditating on this for many years but could not conceive it, could not imagine ever getting a divorce. At the time, I strongly believed that when you marry, you're in it for life. This was an old belief that was born from my early childhood Catholic upbringing, which now created much inner turmoil. I had to get all those parts of me to agree, so I'd have the courage to take that giant step. I was fortunate to have a light circle of my hypnotherapy classmates to support me through this extremely hard time of my life. It gave me the inner strength to go through that door. About a year after we had graduated from hypnotherapy training, our instructors invited us back to a Healing the Healer training in Virginia Beach. The timing was perfect! My husband was against it; he didn't want me to leave for a week. He had not paid attention to what I had been trying to tell him for several months, but now, the message was sinking in, and he realized that he was losing me. I bought my plane ticket, and off I went to spend a week that would totally transform my life. Being reunited with amazing classmates, in the safest environment you can imagine, was the absolute perfect moment to let go of what was and to prepare for what would be. The inner work that we performed during that week was so liberating and empowering. I regained the strength I once had and returned home fully equipped with the tools I needed to face this challenge.

As many of you who have gone through a separation or divorce already know, it's a tough decision to make, no matter how many years you've been together. I would be leaving the life I had for twenty-six years. My entire adult life had been with this man. That was the only life I knew. I would be leaving my house, and it would be the end of all the dreams we shared, all the plans we had made. This was scary on so many levels.

What prevented me from taking that first step for a long time was the thought of being by myself. I had never been by myself. I had grown up with my twelve brothers and sisters by my side, then I started living with my husband soon after I started university. Could I really be on my own? I knew I wanted a different life, but I was scared. Who was going to take care of me now?

The catalyst in helping me through this fear of being alone was the man who eventually became my second husband. I had been teaching monthly meditation classes at a local metaphysical store. One afternoon, about twenty women showed up to my class. Just as we were about to begin, this tall, dark, handsome man with a great smile walked in and asked, "Mind if I join you?" I just about fell off the stool I was sitting on. My heart started beating faster, and my face probably turned several shades of red. "Please do," I answered, while all I could think about was, "where have you been all my life?" It was as if he had just materialized out of nowhere. As he stood there in the doorway, with his long, braided hair draped over his left shoulder, I could imagine myself hopping on the back of his horse and riding off into the sunset. Well, he didn't exactly show up on horseback, but he did have a motorcycle. His appeal was definitely more than just his looks; I felt a sudden jolt throughout my body when I laid eyes on him. I had never experienced anything like that before and have not experienced it since. As soon as I was done teaching the class, I walked over to introduce myself. I had to meet this person that had caused me to have such a powerful reaction. The moment we started chatting, we felt a strong spiritual connection. I found our conversation fascinating, and I wanted more of that. This was something that was lacking in my marriage, and that I had been craving. He represented exactly what I had focused on during my daily meditations. I was head over heels, but there was still the fact that I was married, and he had a girlfriend. After our conversation, life went on as usual, and this fascinating man who had appeared briefly in my life mysteriously vanished. "Why had he been put on my path, then just taken away?" I wondered. "Where had he disappeared to?"

Imagine how ecstatic I was three months later, when I walked into that same store to drop off a flyer for my next workshop, and there he was, the man I had not been able to get out of my mind since the day we met, standing at the counter. I was dancing with joy! He was back, and this time I wasn't going to let him get away. We discovered subsequently that we both had felt that our souls had crossed paths before, something most people would refer to as soul mates. I was head over heels! He had come to rescue me. Be careful what you ask for, you might just get it! The universe really has a great sense of humor.

When the subject of soul mates comes to mind, I am always reminded of what Dr. Wayne Dyer said at one of his lectures that I attended several years ago. "A soul mate is like a turd that won't flush."[2] I have never forgotten those words and have used them in my own lectures because that concept makes perfect sense. I have often heard people say they want to find their soul mate. All I can say is, be careful what you wish for. You see, most people's definition of a soul mate is that special someone who will be their perfect companion, their missing other half, someone who is just like them, and that there is only one soul mate for each of us. That's what I thought at the time, but that's not exactly the case. I discovered that your ideal soul mate is not waiting out there somewhere for you. We can have many soul mates, and we might not see them all as the ideal companion. A soul mate is someone who comes into our life to be our best teacher, to be our mirror, to expose our shadows, and to show us exactly what we are holding on to so that we can let go of it and evolve to a higher state of consciousness. Ask yourself, "is this person showing me an aspect of myself right now? Is this person a reflection of the things I judge? What wisdom have I acquired that I may not have if he or she had not been in my life?" A soul mate will also show you aspects of yourself that you have lost. When you feel attracted to someone, you recognize something in them that has been lost in you but is reawakened in their presence. In that sense, soul mates will come and go throughout our lives, depending on what we need at each moment. However, you are your ideal soul mate. It exists

---

2   Lecture in Naples, Florida, 1995

within you. It is your divine counterpart, your higher infinite self. That is the other half to which we are meant to be united.

Both of my ex-husbands were my soul mates, and so were other friends, family members, and coworkers who have come in and gone out of my life. On one hand, someone may wish to have a spouse, partner, or friend who is always sympathetic and appreciative, which can feed the selfish need of your ego to be appreciated. On the other hand, a soul mate who is unsympathetic and unappreciative will force you to turn within to look at feelings or conditions that cause you to be unhappy. We all play our roles perfectly for a reason, a season, or a lifetime. Sometimes, when one such journey is ending, it can be difficult to accept what is and let go.

The perfect teacher had showed up in my life, at the perfect time, but I didn't recognize the fact at the time. I was in love. I was unaware that I still had so much to learn and overcome emotionally and psychologically. I could not admit this lack of understanding because I strongly believed that I knew what was best for everyone.

I left my first husband, moved out of the beautiful house we had recently bought, and moved in with the new love of my life on the same day. A new and exciting adventure began, and life was great again. We were living in a small apartment, one block from the beach. Every evening, we took walks on the beach to watch the sunset. How romantic is that? I had dreamed of a moment like this, and it was now a reality. Life was like a scene from a movie, and I had the leading role. I had traded the big house, filled with stuff, for a tiny apartment with the bare necessities, but I was so happy. Romance outweighed material possessions.

My hypnotherapy practice was doing well. The response I received from my monthly lectures and workshops was amazing, and more clients were drawn to my practice. It felt wonderful to share my wisdom and to provide the help people were seeking. Since my new partner also had much spiritual wisdom to share, it made perfect sense for us to start teaching classes together, something else I had always dreamed of. It seemed as though everything I had envisioned in meditation was coming true. He brought a great sense of humor, which was a characteristic I lacked. I was always the type to take everything very seriously, so he provided a great balance. We were yin and yang, true life partners who complemented each other. We meditated together daily, we could have deep conversations about the universe and quantum physics, as well as conversations about business and finance. Our friends saw us as the perfect couple. We were living a magical life. We even started a green business in 2004, although there were a few huge bumps, which I will tell you more about later, on the road leading up to that event.

How Did I Get Here?

Was I prepared for what was about to happen on December 26, 2003? Not at all. It was just another sunny afternoon in Fort Myers, Florida, and we decided to go for a motorcycle ride like we did whenever we had the chance. I had spent many hours riding on the back of that motorcycle with my arms wrapped around my knight in shining armor. On a few occasions, he had brought up the idea of getting a motorcycle for me, so we could ride side by side instead of me sitting on the back of his bike. His ex-wife had her own motorcycle, so he thought that's what I would want.

Having spent the last twenty-six years with a man who had almost always decided what was best for both of us, I didn't know how to say no and I thought, "I'm brave; I'll try anything," so I went along with that crazy idea. The next logical step was for me to sign up for motorcycle driving classes, but we had an even better idea. "Why not try driving a motorcycle first to see if I liked it before signing up for classes?"

It was the day after Christmas, so there wouldn't be much traffic; everyone would be relaxing at home. This would be a good time for a trial run. So off we went to find a quiet side road where I could practice driving a motorcycle. When we arrived at a likely spot, we switched places. I was now in the front seat, and he sat behind me. "What have I agreed to?" I thought to myself. This motorcycle was made for a big, strong, six-foot-tall man, not for a five-foot, three-inch, tiny woman. With my hands on the handle bars, I kept thinking, "I can't do this. This bike is way too big and heavy for me. But I have to try, to show him I'm not afraid." Why didn't I listen to my intuition? I wanted to please as usual. I couldn't say no, so I ignored that apprehensive feeling in the pit of my stomach. I had given in and agreed to do something I knew deep down was not right for me.

He put his hands on the outside of mine on the handle bars, and we rode off slowly as he started to teach me all the mechanisms. After driving up and down the road a few times, he thought I had it all under control, so he let go of the handlebars and sat back. That's when I freaked out. The motorcycle started going off the road, and I didn't know how to bring it back. It all happened so fast; he didn't have time to react and grab the handlebars. Within a matter of seconds, I hit a guardrail head-on. The motorcycle fell to the right of the guardrail, and we both landed on the ground to the left. As we fell, my right leg got stuck on the peddle, and the moment I tried to stand up, I knew that my leg was broken below the knee. I had to try to stand up because, on the side of the road in Florida, if you sit too long in one place, the fire ants will find you, and that is definitely an experience you want to avoid. When I did manage to get up, I felt dizzy, and everything went black. All I could see were tiny dots of light flashing all around against a background of darkness. What was happening? I couldn't see. I was terrified and confused. Feeling dizzy, I didn't have any choice but to sit back down, and I don't know how long it took, but my vision eventually started to come back. What a relief! I thought the worst was over.

A few cars drove by. Finally, one driver stopped to see if he could help, and this man immediately called an ambulance. He offered to help my husband put the motorcycle in the back of his truck and then to drive him to meet up with me at the hospital. My husband felt fine and just had a bruise on his left arm, so there was no need for him to be rushed to the emergency.

The ambulance finally arrived, and the paramedics placed me on the stretcher. "We'll take the bike home, and I'll see you at the hospital shortly," I heard my husband say. The moment they laid me down on the stretcher, I could not breathe. The paramedics put the oxygen mask on my face and told me I'd be fine. "Just relax," they said, "it's just a broken leg." I kept trying to convince them that I was not fine, that I really could not breathe, but they didn't pay much attention. It was a very long and terrifying ride, and I wasn't sure I was going to make it. I wanted to shout at them, "can you please drive faster?" but I was totally out of breath.

The next thing I knew, I was on the operating table in the emergency room, and all my clothes were quickly being cut and removed. I remember thinking, "oh, no, why are they cutting my jeans and my new shirt. Is that really necessary?" Then I heard one surgeon say to the other, "we have five minutes to do this, or she's gone." "Was he talking about me? He had to be, because there was no one else in the room. How did I get here?" I thought. It was surreal, absolutely unbelievable. This couldn't be happening. Talk about realizing you're not in control, not the one directing the movie. I never thought anything like that would ever happen to me. They mentioned to me that my husband had arrived, but I had not seen him yet. When they briefed him on my condition, he thought for sure they had the wrong person since he also thought I just had a broken leg.

The surgeon then informed me that he was giving me morphine for the pain but that he could not wait for it to take effect; he had to start the surgery immediately to save my life. I didn't know what surgery he was referring to. This was all happening so fast. They turned me on my left side and said, "this is going to hurt." Within seconds, an incision was made and my ribs were being spread apart so a tube could be inserted. That was the most painful experience of my life. Having your ribs spread apart to make a one-size-fits-all chest tube fit does not qualify as a pleasant experience. I can still hear myself screaming. I thought for sure that I was going to die on that table. The morphine still had not kicked in, and I was being turned over to my right side, and you guessed it: the same procedure had to be done on both sides. This time, I knew what to expect, and I thought, "if I survived the first one, I can make it through this one too."

Once the procedure was over and they moved me to another room, the morphine started having an effect, but my body was rejecting it. I had never taken any medication, not even an aspirin, my entire life. I had always been healthy and never been in the hospital. My system was not liking that substance at all, and it made me sick. Not an enjoyable sensation when you're lying on your back with tubes attached to your body and you can't move.

I was informed of my situation a few hours later, once I was in a more stable condition. I didn't realize how seriously I had been injured, which was probably a good thing at the time, because I might have imagined the worst and panicked. As a result of the accident, I had a broken leg, a broken collarbone, eleven broken ribs, and collapsed lungs. I was told that one lung had collapsed completely, and I had one quarter capacity left in the other one when I arrived at the hospital. No wonder I couldn't breathe and didn't have much time left. My lung cavities had been filling up with fluid, and I was literally drowning in my own fluid.

So it was, on December 26, 2003, I was five minutes away from leaving this earthly plane. A tragic event such as this puts your attention right in the moment, where no other moments exist or matter. Life took on a whole different meaning that day. Eight days in intensive care with tubes connected to several parts of my body gave me plenty of time to reflect. The little picture stuff wasn't so important any more. It's interesting how insignificant all that other stuff can become when breathing has become a matter of life and death, and blood clots are forming in your leg and heading toward your brain, which could be fatal. It puts everything into perspective. Everything else I had been concerned with or worried about until then became irrelevant. All that mattered was being able to take my next breath.

During those eight days in intensive care, the doctor wanted to give me more morphine for the pain, but I said no. I told him I was handling the pain my own way. All those wonderful techniques I had learned in hypnotherapy training became very useful. Just lying there in bed, not able to move, I had plenty of time to focus on healing my body. I had become very skilled at self-hypnosis, and I spent many hours a day in a deep state of calmness and relaxation, focusing all my energy on healing every part of my body that was broken. I visualized each part returning to its original state of perfection with the intention of a full recovery. It was a peaceful outcome, and after eleven days, I was released from the hospital. I was on the road to recovery, but I still had a long hill to climb before I could resume a normal life.

The Next Step of the Journey

Circumstances changed drastically following that ordeal. I was confined to a wheelchair for several months because of the broken leg and broken collarbone. My body was weak, and my lungs would need some time to return to full capacity. My arms felt as heavy as lead. I couldn't lift them up, which made it impossible to get up from the wheelchair or to even roll the wheelchair around the apartment. As much as I tried to stay focused and positive, a deep state of depression came over me, and I couldn't stop crying. This was unfamiliar territory. "What is wrong with me? This is not who I am," I thought. I just kept sinking deeper and deeper down in this dark place, consumed by negative thoughts such as "I'm never going to walk again. I can't even get up and walk around. My life is over.

I'll never be able to return to my normal life. My body is all broken and scarred."

To add insult to injury, literally, the phone calls from collection agencies started coming within one month of my hospital stay. The cost of health insurance was just too expensive to even consider having at the time, and I never thought I was ever going to need it. So, my eleven-day stay at the hospital cost me a total of $165,000.00. How was I going to pay for that? I didn't have that kind of cash just sitting in my bank account. I received invoices from ten different medical institutions, not just from the hospital itself. There were invoices from each physician who attended to the different issues I had: from the broken leg, the broken ribs, the lungs, the blood tests, and so on. One month later, they all wanted to get paid, so they turned the debt over to bill collectors. I don't know if you've ever had to deal with collection agencies, but the rude agents on the other end of the line couldn't care less that I had just had a close call with death and that I was struggling to take my next breath. They just wanted their money. I stopped answering the phone after a few weeks because there was absolutely no reasoning with these people.

I was spiraling down into an overwhelming sadness. This went on for several weeks before I was able to get myself back up to my usual positive state. Accepting what was and remaining in the present moment were my best options. I had to take one step at a time and make decisions. Since it would be a while before I could even get out of the house and could not continue paying the rent on my office space, I had to close my hypnotherapy practice and focus on my own healing. The decision to close my practice was a difficult one. I had worked so hard to achieve this dream of finally living my passion, and now, I had to let it go. Nothing about my life made sense. My dream had been erased.

You would think that this would have been enough, but there was more bad news just around the corner. Exactly four weeks after the accident, I received a call from my husband's supervisor. My husband had returned to work after the accident because he didn't have any broken bones. All he got was a bruise on his left arm, and one of us had to bring in some income. It was late that evening, and I had started to worry that he wasn't home yet. Being confined to the wheelchair, I relied on him for everything. The phone rang around ten o'clock that night. I picked up the phone. It was my husband's supervisor. He said, "there's been an accident at work, and I'm at emergency with your husband." My heart sank, and I started crying. This could not be happening. Not now. "He's going to be okay," he continued, "I'll drive him home as soon as we're done and explain everything."

At midnight, there was a knock at the door. I wheeled myself over to open the door to find my husband standing there with his left arm in a cast. My jaw dropped. He was smiling, and he was okay, but so many horrifying thoughts were going through my mind. He had fallen from about ten feet, and when he had tried to brace himself, his left arm had snapped. When X-rays of his arm were taken following the motorcycle accident, they had missed a diagonal hairline fracture, half way between his shoulder and elbow. The sudden move to brace himself had caused his arm to break where the fracture was, and he had fallen to the ground.

How much more could I endure? I was glad that he was fine. His accident could have been much worse, but who was going to help me now? With one arm how would he be able to push my wheelchair? This eventually turned into a humorous phenomenon. When we met people who knew us but who were unaware of what had happened, the first question they asked was, "who won the fight?" We were quite the vision with me in the wheelchair, one leg in a cast, and him pushing the chair with one arm in a cast. The hilarious comments did help to boost our morale.

I was grateful for my study group friends and my circle of hypnotherapy classmates who continued to surround us with love and light. I found out many years later, at a hypnotherapy class reunion, that my classmates had performed a circle of healing for me when they had heard about the motorcycle accident.

My family was never informed of the seriousness of the accident. The moment I was settled in the intensive care room and my husband was allowed to see me, I asked him to call and let my family know. Because of the collapsed lungs, I didn't have enough breath to speak. I suggested that he call one of my sisters, so she and my brother-in-law could then go over to my mother's house to deliver the news in person. I didn't want my mother to worry. He called and told them about the accident and that I would be okay, but he didn't share with them how seriously I had been injured. They were up in Canada and not just around the corner, able to come by and visit. I didn't know this until several years later when I happened to talk about the accident one day at a family gathering. They never knew how close they had come to losing their baby sister.

There was still the issue of the $165,000.00 medical debt to be paid, and the bill collectors were not going to give up. I grew tired of their threats. I turned within and asked for help. I needed a miracle. In meditation, I focused on help coming my way. I didn't know what help was going to look like, or where it was going to come from, but I surrendered it all to a higher power. I was wrapped in a warm feeling of everything's going to be fine. The next day, I had a strong nudge to call the hospital, and before I dialed the number, I set my intention on reaching the perfect individual who would provide a solution to this problem. It worked. I spoke with the kindest person who listened to my dilemma, and then she offered an incredible solution. She began to tell me about a grant that was available to individuals who earned under a specific amount of money, and she was almost certain that I qualified. She even offered to do all the paper work for me, and she would let me know when she had an answer. The universe had sent an angel to my rescue. Within a week, she called back to give me the great news that I qualified for the grant and that most bills would be covered in full and some would be covered at a percentage. Once the money had been distributed to the collectors, all I had to pay out of pocket was $4,000.00. That, I could handle. I was truly blessed with a miracle that day, and I will be forever grateful. With that burden lifted off my shoulders, I could focus all my attention on healing and getting my strength back.

A New Beginning

Six months later, we were both fully recovered and ready for a new beginning. We decided to move from Florida to Colorado to start a fresh chapter. We were being called to go west, and Colorado seemed appealing to both of us, so we embarked on a new adventure. We didn't know exactly when we would leave or what we would find once we got there, but we were excited to explore the possibilities. We both strongly believed in signs from the universe, and we knew we would be shown each step of the way.

Our life became a series of synchronistic events from the moment we made that decision to go west. For the previous three or four summers, we had attended native American spiritual ceremonies in Idaho. Native American spirituality was of great interest to my husband, and I totally supported it. When we were there that week in July, we shared our plan of moving to Colorado with a lovely woman named Gail who was attending the ceremonies with a few friends, including her doctor. When she told us she was from Colorado, we looked at each other and just about fell off our chairs. We both knew that this person was put on our path for a reason. During the week, we became very close. She shared with us that she had cancer and had come to this ceremony for healing. I told her that I was a hypnotherapist and that I would be glad to help her in any way I could to ease her pain. She was very grateful for the time I spent with her during that week. One evening while we were chatting, she suggested that we move to her ranch in Southern Colorado. She invited us to stay there, at no charge, for as long as we wanted, until we figured out what we wanted to do. "It's a beautiful ranch at the foothills of the Sangre de Cristo Mountains," she said, "with extra living quarters that would be suitable for you two to settle in. I would be delighted to have you there near me."

Without hesitation, we both said yes. Again, the universe had provided us with our next step. We now had a clear destination in mind. We went back to Florida to make the big announcement and started planning our move to Colorado. We kept in touch with Gail during the following weeks to see how she was doing. Each time we spoke with her on the phone, we could hear the excitement in her voice. We had decided on a moving date of August 13, planning to arrive at her ranch on August 16. She was so happy and was counting the days until our arrival.

The day we were scheduled to leave Florida turned out to be an eventful day. It was on a Friday the thirteenth, August 13, 2004, to be exact. Hurricane Charley hit Fort Myers, Florida, as a category four that day. We picked up the rental truck and started loading our belongings to be ready to go early the next morning. Hurricanes are unpredictable, and no one is ever sure in the days ahead where they will specifically make landfall. We didn't think Fort Myers would be on this hurricane's path, so we went ahead as planned, convinced that we would be gone before it arrived on the west coast of Florida. The way hurricanes spin, there will be strong winds, followed by heavy rain, then blue sky, and this pattern continues as the hurricane approaches. Between the periods of rain and blue sky, we managed to load up all our belongings in the truck. We spent our last night in our empty apartment, sleeping on the floor, without electricity or water, listening to the storm wreaking havoc on everything on its path, hoping that the truck and my car would still be intact in the morning.

When we walked outside the next morning, there were fallen trees all over the parking lot of the apartment complex. Several cars were damaged, but miraculously, the rental truck with all our belongings was fine, and so was my car. The entire region was out of power. We needed to fuel the truck before heading out on the road. We had anticipated doing that on the way out of town, but without electricity, none of the gas stations were operational, except for one. We got in line and waited half a day to finally get to the pump. We left Florida several hours behind schedule, watching the mess of Hurricane Charley in the rearview mirror. What a way to leave town! "Let's hurry up and get to Colorado where there are no hurricanes," we thought. With John Denver's Rocky Mountain High playing in the background, we were thrilled to be going west. We called Gail to let her know we would be arriving a bit later than expected because of the storm, but we were on our way.

After driving for a couple of days and delayed by half a day, we didn't want to show up at the ranch in the middle of the night, so we stopped to get a few hours of sleep and arrived early on Monday morning. We drove up the long driveway toward the main house, expecting to see a few familiar faces welcoming us, but no one was around. We walked around, taking in all the breathtaking views of this ranch with the majestic twin peaks mountain in the background. This was a heavenly place with fields of green in all directions, as far as we could see.

A man we didn't know finally came out to greet us. He knew who we were because, apparently, Gail had not stopped talking about us since we had met her in Idaho. He said, "I have some bad news for you, Gail passed away at midnight last night." How could this be? We had talked to her on the phone just the day before. We were devastated. We were so looking forward to hugging her and thanking her for inviting us to live on her ranch. If we had not been delayed by the storm, we would have made it in on Sunday night as planned and would have had time to see her before she passed. Her friend told us that Gail sat in her chair in front of the picture window all day, waiting for us to come up the driveway, telling everyone how excited she was that we were coming. She held on for as long as she could but died in her chair, waiting for us.

Everyone told us we were welcome to stay at the ranch as Gail had intended, but without her there, we didn't feel comfortable moving in. We had never been to Colorado, so we didn't have a clue what to do or where to go. Our money would soon run out, and we had to find a way to generate income. We had developed a great relationship with her doctor friend. He was our age and shared our spiritual views. He had come by to see us and to arrange for Gail's funeral with the other caretakers. Since he knew we were interested in metaphysics, he suggested that we go to Boulder. He was sure we would love it there, that we would fit right in. So, we asked, "where's Boulder? It sounds like the perfect place for us." He showed us on the map and away we went. This was just like a page from *The Celestine Prophecy* by James Redfield. We were following the brightest path and being guided to the next step.[3]

We fell in love with Boulder. Our friend knew we would fit right in. There were metaphysical shops and health food stores everywhere, every type of alternative therapy was available, and people were unique, happy, and healthy. Its location in the foothills of the Rocky Mountains made it a hiking paradise. We went on many road trips, just exploring the area. It was such a fascinating and unusual place—unlike any other town we had ever seen. Our favorite saying became, "Only in Boulder!" On one of our trips, just north of Boulder, we noticed a house built exactly like a pyramid. It was so intriguing. Each time we drove by, we always wondered what it looked like inside.

A few months later, we were invited to join an Edgar Cayce study group in Lyons, not far from Boulder. I was a member of the Edgar

---

3 The book is a first-person narrative of spiritual awakening. The narrator is in a transitional period of his life and begins to notice instances of synchronicity, which is the belief that coincidences have a meaning personal to those who experience them.

Cayce Association, so the association had informed the local group that we were now living in the area and that we might be interested in joining it. We thought it would be a great way to make new friends. The Boulder group happily welcomed us, and we had an instant connection with one individual in particular. After a couple of weekly meetings, he invited us for dinner at his house the following weekend. Then he told us where he lived. Yes, you guessed it. He lived in the pyramid house. This was another unbelievable, synchronistic moment! We became great friends and spent many wonderful evenings in the pyramid house. What an incredible place. Only in Boulder!

That house would become the next link of the journey. Our friend invited us to a presentation held at his house, where we were introduced to a man who was starting a new venture and was looking for representatives to help promote his idea. We were looking for a source of income, so this was perfect timing. We joined his team and worked with him for a few years. During that time, we were introduced to an entrepreneurial association and attended several classes a year where we learned how to start a business.

Our Dream Business

Through our networking activities, we became well-known among investors and entrepreneurs. It was time to start our own business. We wanted to create a business that would allow us to travel, make a difference in the lives of people and the planet, and be lucrative. Our dream business of replanting tropical rainforests around the world was born. The projects we were developing were in amazing places in the world, one of them being Indonesia, where we were fortunate to spend a couple of days on the island of Borneo with orangutans. From the time that I was a little girl, I had fantasized about being in the presence of a wild animal and what it would feel like. Having been raised on a farm, I've always been an animal lover, but the dream of playing with a wild animal, that was a passion like no other. So, imagine my reaction when I found myself in the rainforest, surrounded by sixty or so young, orphaned orangutans. The word orangutan means man of the forest. They are just like us, the only difference is that they can't talk, but they understand everything. Most of the adult orangutans had been killed by illegal loggers, who were cutting down the trees, destroying the rainforest, and killing the orangutans who just got in their way. The babies were left behind. The main objective of this project was to help rebuild their natural habitat.

We spent a month in Jakarta, meeting with our local business partners and developing our plan. Then, we all went to the island of Borneo for two days to see how the project would be implemented. When we arrived on location, I was in awe to see the orangutans all around us. As I walked in and sat slowly on the ground, I thought to myself, "I can't believe this is happening. I am so grateful to be here." This was a whole new experience, in unfamiliar territory. It took only a few seconds for the orangutans to notice me, and they started approaching, curious to see this new person who seemed quite friendly. Two of them climbed on my lap without hesitation and started hugging me like they were never going to let go. Before long, a few more joined in, and they were climbing all over me, wanting to take turns being in my arms. They behaved like two-year-old human children, very playful, rolling around, curious about everything. A group of them hung on to me all day, as if they had found a new mom.

When we walked through the forest, I had one on each side, holding my hands, two more clinging to my legs, and one hugging me with her arms and legs wrapped around my neck and waist. Their legs are like an extra set of arms. So, when you try to remove their arms from around you, their legs grab onto you. Impossible to win against four arms! One would try to pull another one down, so it could take its turn in my arms. I remember thinking at that moment, "I must be in heaven. I have accomplished a precious childhood dream. I am walking in the forest, holding hands with wild animals." So fascinating! That was one of the most memorable moments of my life. What a thrilling experience! If that had been my last day on earth, I would have died happy.

Evidently the business we were building looked very promising, exciting, and rewarding for everyone involved, especially the planet, and, of course, the orangutans, but it all came to a halt in 2009, following the crash of the United States economy. All our projects were put on hold, and, of course, the investments stopped.

Our dream ended. We had put all of our efforts and money into building the business, and now it was going nowhere. We lost our house to foreclosure and all our savings, which had gone into the business. We decided to move back to Florida to be closer to my husband's son and grandson. We struggled for about another year until we could no longer contend with the financial difficulties of this situation. We had accepted a very strenuous job on the road, just to survive, but we were barely earning a living. After six months, I couldn't keep going. This state of affairs had put so much emotional and financial stress on both of us. All the beautiful moments we had shared over the past eight years were replaced with hatred, anger, frustration, and resentment. We could barely look at each other. There were no more conversations. We seemed broken on so many levels. Our dream was over and so was our marriage. The sadness was unbearable. I felt completely alone.

Just when I thought I had it all figured out, after so many amazing life experiences, my spiritual path had led me to this? This was where I would end up? What happened? I didn't understand any of it. Apparently, I still had more to learn, and I still wasn't clear about my purpose. I now had another major life decision to make. I had to get out of this situation but had no idea what to do. I had nothing left—no home to go to, and no money. I felt trapped. When circumstances reach such a low and painful level, when you've reached rock bottom, there's nowhere to go but up, which forces you to reach within to find the power to make new choices. I turned to my dad for help as I cried myself to sleep one night. My dad passed away in 1996, but that night I felt his comforting presence around me, and I asked him what to do. The next day, on my birthday, in November 2010, I received a call from my mom, wishing me happy birthday, which she then followed with, "Why don't you come back to Canada?" With tears running down my face, I knew, and I replied, "yes, that's what I'm going to do. I am going back to Canada. I will see you soon." I was not alone after all; my dad was there as my spirit guide that night. I had no idea when and how I was going to do this, or what I was going to do once I got there, I just knew, without a doubt, it had to be my next step.

Two weeks later, my husband and I drove to Virginia Beach to meet with my sister and brother-in-law, who had driven down from Canada to pick me up. It was the halfway point between Florida and Ontario, Canada. This is where my husband and I parted ways after an eight-year relationship. We transferred what was left of my belongings, basically my clothes and a few other items, from one vehicle to the other. We hugged and said good-bye. That was it! It all happened in a matter of minutes.

The twenty-hour drive north from Virginia Beach was filled with so many mixed feelings, so many thoughts spinning around in my head. Extreme sadness, followed by moments of freedom and exhilaration. It had all happened so fast. I didn't really know how to process what I was feeling. I was heading north, and he was heading south. I didn't know if or when I was going to see him again. Was it really over? I had so many unanswered questions.

Starting Over

Just like that, I found myself back in Canada after living in the United States for twenty-one years. Never saw that one coming! I felt like Dorothy in the *Wizard of Oz*, like I had just been twirled around in a tornado, and when it stopped, everything was gone, the scenery was completely different. I literally had been transported to another country! Life as I had known it for the past twenty-one years no longer existed. If someone had told me a few years before that I would be living back in Canada in 2010, I would have thought they were crazy. My plan was to live in the United States for the rest of my life.

In a matter of a few weeks, my life completely flipped upside down, or is it right side up? I found myself without a spouse, without a business, financially bankrupt, homeless with only a few items left in storage, and without a job. A very strange feeling indeed. I had never expected to find myself in such a place in my early fifties. Another how did I get here moment. I never thought this would happen! This was not part of my plan, not at all what I had envisioned in my daily meditations. Doesn't that all sound familiar?

As if all that wasn't enough, three weeks after returning to Canada, my mother passed away. I am grateful to have spent the last three weeks of her life by her side, and she was so happy that her wish for her baby to come back home had been fulfilled. I am also so grateful for my loving family. Being back in my country, I was surrounded with my brothers and sisters. They were so supportive; I don't know what I would have done without them. They really took great care of their baby sister. One of my sisters provided me with a place to stay while I figured out my next step, and for that, I will be forever grateful. Another sister gave me clothes. Coming from Florida, I needed warmer clothes, especially in December. When I moved back to Florida from Colorado the previous year, I donated my winter clothes, as I was not going to need them. A the time I had no plans of ever living in a cold climate again. Another sister gave me all the furniture I would need to furnish my apartment a few months later, which I still appreciate to this day.

This was the transition I needed, the bridge between the story that had just ended and the new one that was now beginning. Being surrounded with so much love gave me the strength to put my life back together again. My family was my circle of light. There were times when I felt overwhelmed with sadness, having lost everything and then losing our mom shortly after. How did I get here? What happened? What would I do now?

From the day I was born, I had never been on my own. I firmly believed that to be happy, I needed a spouse. That was the only way I knew. Being alone did not exist as a possibility in my reality. I had never experienced that. I had been very attached to my family, and then, to each of my spouses. I thought that the only way I could live was with someone always by my side. My new reality was now to learn to be okay and happy all by myself, whether I would ever be in a relationship again. I had to become my own soul mate and best friend.

Not only had my outside world changed completely and drastically, I found my inner world was changing as well. Even though meditation had played an important part of my life for thirty years, I no longer had any desire to meditate. That was gone too. I had been so dedicated to my daily meditation practice. I had rarely missed a day. It had been such a great instrument in learning about myself and in overcoming emotional baggage. I had experienced many amazing moments during meditation. My self-improvement practices had lost their meaning and importance. Beliefs that had been deeply ingrained in my mind were disappearing and being replaced with new thoughts such as maybe people and the world didn't need to be saved. Maybe they were exactly the way they were supposed to be, and it was not up to me to save them or help them reach their potential. Everything about my life was different, and I didn't understand what was happening.

When you have nothing left, all you can do is live one moment at a time. Giving up was not an option; I had to get back on my feet. The first thing I wanted to do was find work, so I could start rebuilding my life. I dedicated my days to focusing on getting work, and within a few months, I found a job and relocated to a new city.

That felt good, priorities one and two were taken care of. I had a job and an apartment I could call my own. For the first time in my life, I was living by myself, and I was comfortable with that.

With my immediate needs in check, life was looking brighter, but it still felt so strange to be going through all these changes. There were many more questions, and I wanted answers. Thoughts of being in control still had a strong hold on me, even after everything I had been through in the past few years, but, increasingly, I was realizing that I was not in control in the way I understood it at the time.

CHAPTER 3

STEPPING OUT OF MY COMFORT ZONE

When you're ready to hear a message, it always appears; that's how it has always been for me anyway. But you must pay attention, and remain open to all the interesting ways the message can be delivered. It might come through something you hear on the radio or while you're watching a movie. Sometimes your social media page will open up to the perfect quote someone just posted. The message can even appear in huge letters on a billboard. The signs are everywhere. I've even had them show up on the license plate of the car in front of me in traffic. There are no limits to how the answers to your questions can appear. I don't know how it happens for you, but for me, it usually comes from the perfect book I happen to be reading at the moment. The timing always fascinates me. It seems that each time I'm faced with a challenge and wonder what it all means, I come across a passage in a book that makes me go, "ah, now I get it. That makes perfect sense." That's what happened to me when I was going through this unfamiliar life experience. I came across an e-book entitled *Butterflies are Free to Fly, A New and Radical Approach to Spiritual Evolution* by Stephen Davis. That book had the perfect message for me at that very moment. I needed a new and radical approach to my spiritual evolution because nothing made sense anymore. The author's life experiences resembled mine in many ways, and reading about them helped me understand what I was going through. I was at the next step of my journey, and after reading that book, I knew that everything was just fine. I was just fine. It helped me transition through this chapter of my life. I wanted to be able to let go of what my life had been, accept what was, and to have faith in what would be. I became as free as a butterfly, which was exactly the state of mind I needed to be in to know that I wasn't going crazy.

Perhaps you're having one of those moments right now, reading this book. If so, you are proving my point! You are receiving exactly what you need, when you need. The universe does look after you.

Now Is a Good Time to Start

Every time I shared my life experiences with someone, their reaction was, "what you went through is incredible, you should write a book." I admit that the thought of writing my story was very appealing. It was something I had considered on several occasions, and I had started jotting down a rough outline in a notebook, but the idea of actually turning these notes into a manuscript seemed so far-fetched. Even though I knew better than to entertain negative thoughts such as "you're not good enough to write a book," or "who am I to think I have what it takes to be an author?" I still listened to them. It was an idea I kept putting off to someday, when all the stars and planets lined up. Then I would do it. I usually thought something like, "right now, I'm too busy and not in the right place, physically, or mentally." That was that, and a few more years went by.

After I moved into my first apartment, I happened to look through an old notebook and noticed that I had written "start where you are with what you have, and do it." At this point in my life, while I was thrilled to have my own place, I wanted to have a bigger apartment that would be more conducive to writing. I had every intention of getting back to writing once I had a more suitable place. The old familiar thought process of "when I have that I'll be able to do that" continued to pop into my head, and I put off writing my book, still waiting for when I was in that better place. When, in the spring of 2017, I got the urge to open up my notes again and read the ideas I had written down, I realized that perhaps I should follow my own suggestions.

I thought, "while I'm waiting for my penthouse apartment with a view of the river to show up, I can start where I am with what I have. Why not pay attention to my own words, and do it?" As I sat with my laptop on my knees, reading my notes, it all became clear how I could rearrange the furniture, and make use of what I already had. You would have thought I was moving; I was so excited. Without a doubt it felt like the absolute right thing to do. My main goal was to place my desk where I would have the best light, could set up my laptop, and be ready to write at any moment. So that afternoon, I decided to rearrange my living room, moving all the book shelves, the sofa, the chairs, and my precious antique desk. That desk and my meditation chair were the two items I had kept after losing everything seven years before. They meant too much to me to sell them, and I'm so glad I kept them. Over the years, thousands of hours had been spent meditating in that chair, and my antique desk was where I kept all my cherished items, notes, and crystals, but I had hardly used it because of where it was placed in my small apartment. It faced a kitchen wall, and the lighting wasn't good. Not so inspiring.

In all the years I had been in this apartment, I never thought it would be possible to arrange my living-room furniture any other way than how I had first placed it. It seemed like the only way the furniture could work in a tight space. Once I started moving things around, it all came together quite miraculously. I found the perfect spot, with natural light, for the desk, and I ended up surrounded by my crystals and books and my meditation chair, of course. Adding an essential oil diffuser completed my sacred space. I was ready to write my book. I used what I had, where I was, and created a more ideally suited environment for writing. That weekend, I wrote over seven thousand words. Nothing like following your own advice.

Stepping Out Even Further

As I wrote this chapter of the book, I was going through a time during which I distanced myself from social events and people, and I wondered what that was all about. Socializing and dating had taken up most of my weekends since my divorce, and now, I was finding myself losing interest in all that and just wanting to be alone. For someone who had spent most of her life never wanting to be alone, that's exactly what I now preferred. There were many changes going on at work, resulting in an unsettled feeling. I just wanted to be by myself and focus on what I needed to do. I felt like I had lost my way, and my life was going nowhere. Even my dreams were trying to communicate that message. A few times a week, I would have similar dreams that were symbolic of having lost my way.

When I opened my social media page that day, the following quote appeared at the top of the page: "[t]here's a sacred energy guiding you. That's why lately you've been distancing yourself from who and what no longer serves you. Instead you've now begun attracting and manifesting who and what does serve you, elevate you, nourish and inspire you to vibrate higher daily." I am always fascinated at how these messages show up, and I am grateful for the sacred energy that guides me. It does, however, require patience and a sense of humor.

Whenever I receive a message that speaks to me so profoundly and accurately, I pay attention because I know I'm being led to the next step of the journey. So, what was I ready to attract in my life that would nourish and inspire me?

My financial situation had been weighing heavily on my mind for some time. My salary covered all my living expenses, but it was not really enough to build any kind of retirement plan. Most people my age were retiring, but here I was, still having to work and not seeing how I could possibly ever get to retirement. I had to find a way to create the financial freedom that would allow me to get out of this rat race and be able to live life on my terms.

Within a few weeks, an advertisement for a course in an investment field that I had been interested in for many years just popped up in front of me, and I knew that I wanted to enroll. I didn't know all the details but decided to sign up for the introductory presentation. That first step led to stepping out of the comfort zone I had been in for the past seven years and entering a whole new world. It was both scary and exciting at the same time because I was doing this by myself, with no other human to bounce ideas off of. No one in my family, circle of friends and acquaintances were familiar with this field of study. I trusted the guidance of the sacred energy, and I decided to enroll in this course. I've always enjoyed adding new skills to my toolbox, and I was ready for this new adventure.

Three or four months into this new venture, I began to wonder what I had been thinking when I signed up for these classes. I would come home from work, take classes in the evening—sometimes until midnight, then go back to work the next day. I remember feeling totally frustrated and so overwhelmed that I thought about quitting and asking for my money back. Then I came across a quote that a friend had posted online, "[t]o that one soul reading this, I know you're tired, you're fed up, you're close to breaking, but there's strength within you, even when you feel weak. Keep going." It doesn't get much clearer and to the point that that! I felt like that message had been written just for me, exactly when I needed it.

Just in case I needed more reinforcement to conquer this new challenge, which I absolutely did; a few months later, I read these words from another friend, "[d]on't be afraid of new beginnings, from new people, new energy, new surroundings, new challenges.

Embrace it!" Help is always close by; we just have to remember to pay attention.

To Meditate or Not to Meditate

As I mentioned previously, I had lost the desire to meditate after my life was completely turned upside down. At first, I was quite puzzled that a daily practice, which had been such a significant aspect of my life for so many years, had lost its meaning and importance. How could that be? I also wondered if it had just all been a waste of time because my life didn't manifest all those wonderful situations that I had spent so much time focusing on during the many hours and years of meditation. The dreams I had manifested had all fallen apart.

One day, the light came on, and I knew that it had not been a waste of time. There was nothing wrong with me. I had simply arrived at the next step on the ladder.

Meditation was not about being more spiritual, not about manifesting more stuff in my life. Meditation was and is about achieving a state of being that is already within me. It's about creating a space where you can listen to your inner wisdom, get to know your mind, and see reality as it is. It's about changing your relationship with your thoughts and realizing that you are not your thoughts. Thoughts will come and go, and you don't have to hold on to them or have an opinion about them. There is no need for an internal commentator to analyze every thought. Meditation is about changing your frequency and becoming who you really are.

In that moment, I realized that I was becoming that person I had aspired to be during my hours of meditation—the person who desired to live in the moment, to be at peace in each moment, in each situation, that person who could let go and trust the process, which is exactly what I had to do following the accident, and then again after losing everything, and moving back to my native country. I had been so set in my ways, convinced that I always knew best for myself and for everyone else, and the universe had provided ideal opportunities for me to realize that. Life learning moments don't always have to be that extreme, but I guess extreme was necessary for me to pay attention.

I didn't need to sit in a special place, in a special way, with my hands placed in a certain way, for one hour every morning to connect with my infinite consciousness. The sensation I used to experience during meditation was in me; it was me. For most of my years of meditation, the peaceful feeling would fade away shortly after the hour was over. When I realized that it remained alive within me and that I could just be that serene person in all situations throughout the day, that was my Aha! moment. I had achieved that state of consciousness, that awareness of choosing how to react to whatever happened in each moment. Even though I sometimes still get anxious or impatient about the future, I can quickly remind myself to stay in the present. It is a learning process, and the more I remind myself that I can choose how to react to a situation, the more natural it becomes. We have the free will to choose in each moment.

I remember thinking about the kind of person my father was. As far as I had observed since I was a child, he always reacted to situations in a loving way. He was always calm and peaceful, and he seemed happy all the time. Always a smile, never a frown. Nothing made him angry; I never saw him get upset, not even when my brothers behaved in crazy, hilarious ways. Everybody loved him. I'm not saying he was perfect, but he was a kind soul, the kindest soul I've ever known. He was my role model, and I admired who he was. A serene individual who enjoyed each moment, but yet, he never meditated. I used to wonder how that was possible because I thought that the only way to achieve such a state of being was by spending many hours in meditation. How did he do it?

"Life is ten percent what happens to you and ninety percent how you react to it,"[4] is a quote by Charles R. Swindoll that I had read and

4 https://www.brainyquote.com/quotes/charles_r_swindoll_388332

heard on several occasions, but somehow it had not quite registered in my mind, like it didn't apply to me. That one day when the light came on, I got it. That was what it's all about. Circumstances don't matter. How you choose to respond or react in each moment is what determines your state of being, not the circumstances. That's it! That's all you have to do, and to do that you have to be awake with your eyes open. Our physical reality is the perfect place to apply the wisdom of daily meditation.

This thought reminds me of the story of the Farmer's Donkey: A Fable for Our Time:

> "One day a farmer's donkey fell down into an abandoned well. The animal whined for hours as the farmer tried to figure out what do do. The farmer concluded that since the donkey was old and the well was dry, it wasn't worthwhile saving this animal. So, the farmer asked his neighbors to come over and help him cover up the well. They grabbed shovels and began throwing dirt into the well.
>
> At first, the frightened donkey cried horribly, but he soon quieted down. When the farmer looked down the well to see what was happening, he was surprised to discover that, with every shovel of dirt that fell on his back, the donkey would shake it off and take a step up.

Before long, the donkey was able to step up over the edge of the well and happily trot away.

Moral: Life is going to shovel dirt on you. The trick to getting out of the well is to shake it off and take a step up. Every adversity can be turned into a stepping stone. The way to get out of the deepest well is by never giving up but by shaking yourself off and taking a step up. What happens to you isn't nearly as important as how you react to it."[5]

So, yes meditation helps you focus your mind and achieve great states of consciousness. When you tune in to this higher frequency, it feels wonderful, but how you apply it in your everyday life is what matters. It's not about escaping this reality for another; it's about being in this world fully. It's about understanding our mind and engaging in this reality, here and now. We are here to experience life in a physical, three-dimensional world, and it's up to us how we choose to live in it. We can get distracted by being so focused on our goal that we miss what is right in front of us. "The Monkey Business Illusion", an experiment conducted by cognitive psychologists Daniel J. Simons and Christopher Chabris in 1999, demonstrates how people can focus so hard on something that they become blind to the unexpected, even when staring right at it.

Enjoy the world you are in now. It's not necessary to spend hours in meditation to get what you desire. Remember there are no rules, nothing you should do or must do. Thinking you should do something implies that you are wrong for not doing it. Replacing *should* with *could* allows you the freedom to choose to do something. We've been brainwashed into thinking that to manifest what we want we must follow certain rules and rituals. It's not necessary to smudge yourself with sage or burn incense or wear amulets. You can if you want to or if it's meaningful to you and helps you achieve a deeper connection to your inner self, but you don't have to. Your physical body is all you need. It's already a giant receiver and transmitter of energy. You can imagine a circle of white light around you before starting your meditation, and some people find it useful to call on spirit guides for protection. Do not let these rituals become a form of religion. Allow yourself to simply be—be with your breath—that's what matters.

5   https://rablinsingh.wordpress.com/2014/01/07/ the-farmers-donkey-a-fable-for-our-time/

Don't feel guilty for not meditating every day or for not being able to meditate long enough, not getting it right, or for not meditating at all. It's perfectly fine. I stopped meditating for seven years and realized that it's okay to take a break now and then. Life happens in cycles. It has been scientifically proven that our minds and the cells in our bodies change every seven years. There's a time to work and a time to rest, a time to ride the energy of a cycle and a time to go within and wait for the next one.

During that seven-year period, I was given plenty of opportunities to see that I was still holding on to some baggage. That time allowed me to focus on what was right in front of me, and by paying attention to my reactions, I continued to be transformed. This break also allowed me to let go, be less serious, and just have fun. After everything I had been through, I just wanted to let go and dance for a while.

At the end of those seven years, my life had fallen into a rut, leaving me feeling anxious and unfulfilled. When a new cycle begins, the natural release of energy will nudge you to move forward and make changes. I started having a series of dreams that indicated that I had lost my way. I recognized the theme because I had had almost identical dreams many times before, so I knew what they meant. It was a message to start meditating again and to reawaken to my inner wisdom. Today, I have made a few adjustments to my meditations. They are more focused on discovering who I am and on raising my vibrational frequency, allowing the better me to shine through.

As your frequency changes, what is meant for you will show up. The universe responds to your frequency. Look at meditation as a joyful and inquisitive way to discover who you are. If you approach it as just another task to add to your already too busy schedule or as something to do because it's supposed to be good for you, it's probably best not to meditate.

A Simple Meditation Exercise

Meditation does not have to be complicated. The most frequent comments I hear from people are, "my mind won't shut down; I can't stop all these thoughts from coming in. How do you clear your mind?" We've all experienced this, in daily life as well as in meditation. One thought comes in, it leads to another and another, and a succession of thoughts follows, as if they're somehow connected like chain links. For example, I hear the sound of the refrigerator in my apartment. I wish it would stop because it's so annoying and distracting, and then I wonder when the landlord will do something about it, and perhaps I should move to a better apartment. When I win the lottery, I can move. Oh, yes! I have to remember to scan my ticket tomorrow. Ah, but the forecast calls for rain all day tomorrow, so I'll go straight to the office. I hope it stops raining by the time I go to that lecture at the library tomorrow night. It should be a good one; astral travel is an exciting subject. I know they will be asking us to sign up for their classes after the lecture. Not sure if I want to do that. It means getting out of downtown in the five o'clock traffic. It might be a great occasion to meet like-minded people, but winter is just around the corner, and I don't really want to drive in snowstorms. Your thoughts keep going and going in a loop, and you wonder how you ever got from a noisy refrigerator to driving in a snowstorm. It is possible to change your relationship with your thoughts.

Steps to a simple meditation exercise:[6]

1. Find a place where you will not be disturbed. You can lie down or sit in a comfortable chair or on a cushion on the floor, whatever works for you. I prefer to have calm, relaxing music playing in the background or through headphones, but it's not necessary.

---

6   Grzela, Jocelyne. Simple meditation exercise. 2020. https://jocelynegrzela.com/meditations

2. Once you're comfortable, close your eyes, and take a few deep breaths; this will signal your body to relax. Your breath is your doorway between levels of consciousness. As you breathe in, you can say something like, "I accept divine love and guidance." Encircle yourself with the white light of divine love and protection, and if you wish, invite your spirit guides to join you in your sacred space.

3. Then focus on each part of your body, starting at your feet. Pay attention to sensations such as tingling, pulsating, and numbness. Continue moving up your legs and hips, then along the back side of your body, up to your shoulders and down your arms and hands. Simply observe the sensations and notice any feelings, without analyzing. Whether the sensation is pleasant or unpleasant, just feel it. You can imagine a warm, soothing energy flowing through each part of your body.

4. As mentioned above, thoughts will come in and out. Thoughts are just like clouds floating by; don't get attached to them. There is no need to react or change anything. Let them float by; behind the clouds, there is a vast and clear blue sky. Be still and be in harmony with what is. If your mind wanders, release the thinking, relax, and return to your breath and to scanning your body. I find that bringing my focus back to what I call the black space between my eyes brings me instantly to that peaceful, quiet state of being.

5. Continue scanning your body from your shoulders up to the back of your neck, to the top of your head, feeling any sensations, then move down to your forehead and relax every part of your face, the small muscles around your eyes, relaxing your jaw, which tends to naturally release the chatter going on in your mind. Then continue moving down the front of your

body, to your chest and your abdomen, and back down your legs, all the way down to your feet.

6. When you have scanned your entire body and can feel the heaviness of your arms and legs, just be still in the silence of meditation. When you quiet the mind, you can hear or sense the answers you seek. Compare your mind to water in a pond. If you constantly stir the water in the pond, sediment will rise up, float around, and cloud up the water. If you let the water be, sediment will slowly settle to the bottom, and the water will return to being clear. If you allow your mind to rest in that place of awareness, your mind will naturally become clear.

7. Then count yourself down backward, slowly, from ten to one, going deeper with each number. If it helps, you can imagine yourself walking down a beautiful staircase as you count down. By the time you reach the last step, imagine yourself in a beautiful garden or sitting by a river or in any other special place that is meaningful to you.

8. There are no perfect words to say. Use what works for you; create your own mantra; and feel the meaning of the words. I sometimes repeat the following words as I enter into the silence:
   Be still and know that I am God (use whatever words that work for you, all that is, infinite spirit, infinite intelligence, the presence, source energy, sacred energy, divine energy, divine spirit, universal wisdom, etc.)
   Be still and know that I am
   Be still and know
   Be still
   Be
   Be with your breath. Be here now. At first, you will find

yourself thinking about your breathing, then move into feeling it, then just be your breath. If your mind wanders, repeat your mantra. You can also imagine placing each thought on a leaf, and letting it float down the river.

9. Once you enter the silence, it is the moment to ask what you seek answers to. It is best to ask open-ended questions such as "what do I need to know about that situation, that person?" or "will you show me my next step?" If there is something you desire in your life, you can state something like, "divine spirit, open the way for me or the (insert your desire), let all that is mine by divine right now reach me." Be in that state of awareness for as long as you desire.

10. Then, express gratitude for the information you have received. Notice the feeling in your heart center, and imagine a warm, brilliant light pulsating and filling your entire heart area. This light expands to every part of your body. Now, imagine the light reaching out to all your loved ones, out to your neighborhood, your city, your country, and beyond, out to the entire planet, then out to the universe. Then bring it back to your heart center.

11. When you are ready, simply take a deep breath, and you will come back to conscious awareness. That's all.

The answers you seek may come in the silence of meditation, or they might come at a later time, when you go about your day, and they can come in many different ways. If you don't get an answer during meditation, it could be because other steps need to happen before you can have access to the answer. Just remember to pay attention to all the details as you interact with your environment. Be patient; we spend a lot of time asking, and we forget how important it is to take the time to listen. Some messages may appear to be just coincidences.

Something else I have realized about meditation is that it's not about trying to re-create an amazing experience that you once had, so don't worry if you can't return to that same feeling. Meditation is an ever-changing process. I still remember an amazing experience I had several years ago, during a two-hour meditation that seemed like it went by in twenty minutes. I truly found myself in a perfectly clear, blissful state, just consciousness that felt as expansive as the entire universe. I was so deeply focused that nothing else seemed to exist, no awareness of my physical body, no awareness of time or space, and no thoughts at all. I would describe it as entering the void, where I lost all sense of my individual identity and became one with the universe. What an experience! No words exist to describe what I felt. I remember being in a state of total bliss that entire day. I floated in a bubble of oneness and felt only pure love toward everyone I met. I have had other wonderful moments in meditation such as floating up through the earth's grid and going through a door, then flying above a forest of silver trees. I still remember these moments fondly; they are truly out of this world! When such moments happen, we want to experience them again, and we try to reproduce them during our next meditation, but we must remember that there is only this moment, right now. Meaningful moments like these may remain with you for hours or days or years, but don't feel discouraged if or when they fade away. Feel joyful each time you reawaken to such inspirational moments.

Meditation is about your state of being in this present moment. You will feel the benefits of meditation throughout the day and throughout your life. It will help you overcome stories you've been holding on to and help you change your habitual tendencies to react to what happens around you. You will remain aware without reacting mindlessly.

I'm getting to know the real me. In the same way that I remain focused and present during meditation, I do my best to remain fully present and aware throughout the day. If my mind wanders, whether during meditation or during my daily activities, I bring my attention back to just being present again. The same principles apply everywhere all the time. Be still and allow your divine self to show you the truth you seek.

Know that there is more than one way and one place to meditate. You can meditate anywhere, anytime—while at work, while standing in line at the store, while playing a musical instrument, while painting, or while walking or dancing—by simply inhaling and exhaling with awareness and relaxing with each exhalation. Each time that you simply focus on your breathing, you are meditating. Be your breath. If you want to become more mindful or more present during meditation, you must try to develop your visual ability in your normal life. Wherever you are, whether you are walking to work or taking a walk in nature, observe your surroundings as if your eyes are a video camera. Pay attention to all the details, and interact with what is around you. This practice will help you become more present in your daily life and in meditation.

Each one of us is responsible for our own inner development. Only by practicing meditation will you know if it is beneficial and relevant in your life. Noticing how you respond to circumstances in your life will tell you that you have changed. Do what works for you. Meditation is meant to be a joyful experience. If sitting out in nature brings you joy, do that. If spending time with your pet brings you joy, do that. If playing a musical instrument or painting brings you joy, do that. If going to church brings you joy, do that. If you find that reciting or repeating passages and scripture has become rote memorization instead of uplifting, bring yourself back to the present moment, put life into it. Take a look at what you are doing; if what you're doing feels like a heavy task, perhaps it's time for a change.

CHAPTER 4

ALLOWING

For so many years, I thought I was in control of my life, and I created, manifested, whatever you want to call it, what I wanted. I lived The Secret and the Law of Attraction. I even taught classes on this subject long before it was popular. Oh, and I succeeded in getting most of these wishes. I fulfilled my dream of being a hypnotherapist, attracted the perfect partner, created the perfect business, lived amazing adventures, then lost it all. I've had my life turned upside down and came close to leaving this earth plane.

Where did I go wrong? After devoting so many years of my life making my dreams happen, I felt like a failure. My wishes came through, but they didn't last. I didn't understand why I wasn't getting everything I wanted, my way, when I wanted it. How come other people were achieving their dreams, and I was not? Not getting what I wanted left me feeling sad and depressed.

So, I asked, "if there's something for me to learn in all this, what is it?" The answer I received was that I had missed one very important aspect about manifesting. I was not living in the moment, not being happy in the moment; instead, I lived for the time when that manifestation would happen. My ego had put conditions on my happiness. When such and such happens, I will be happy. When

I meet the perfect partner, I will be happy. When I get this thing I want, then I can do this other thing, and life will be great. When I have enough money, I can buy that beautiful condo and be happy. When I have enough of this thing, then I can be this. You get the picture. I was always living for that moment *when*. Therefore, I was sad, anxious, or discouraged until that desired moment arrived. Sometimes, the desire never materialized or when I finally met that perfect partner or had enough money to buy a house, I lost them. I didn't understand why. Why weren't my wishes being fulfilled? I was doing everything I thought I was supposed to do. I was visualizing my goal during meditation; I was focusing on it all day long; I had a vision board and had positive affirmations posted on my bathroom mirror and throughout the house to remind me of it. Some of you are probably smiling now because you've done the same things. What was I doing wrong? Why wasn't it working? Why wasn't I getting what I wanted? What was I missing?

Detaching from the Outcome of Your Desire

Having desires is wonderful. Have as many as you like. All desires are good since they all come from the divine mind. It's natural and exciting to have desires. What I finally understood is that intention is not something you do; it is a field of consciousness to which you are always connected. Not only are you always connected; you are the field. That is how spirit expresses itself through you. Visualizing your plan brings you in alignment with the state of consciousness and puts you on the same frequency to receive the fruit of your plan. But the physical mind is not designed to know how or when something is going to happen. It's designed to perceive and react to what shows up on your path.

The physical mind is limited and sometimes misinterprets the desire; therefore, it has its own selfish agenda. Humans are masters of limitations. We allow our judgments, beliefs, opinions, and fears to get in our own way. By telling the higher mind what, how, and when we want this desire, we are not allowing it to express itself through us. Instead, we are imposing limitations on the plan and putting the plan in a box, which is exactly what I did. My plan had to look the way I pictured it, and it had to happen when I decided it should. I gave God a shopping list. The physical mind doesn't see the bigger picture; it is only aware of a small piece of it. You have probably heard this expression before, "if you want to make God laugh, tell Him your plans." Being a spiritual being means surrendering your plan to divine perfection. Surrender and trust that everything is just the way it's supposed to be. This was a tough lesson for me to learn. This was too unfamiliar to my ego, and my ego was not ready to accept that.

The key, I learned, is to not be attached to the outcome of your desire, to have zero expectation of the outcome, and to appreciate everything. Allow the higher mind to express itself through you, and accept what comes. Your higher self will show you signs that will let you know, without a doubt, what you need to see and hear. Be open to all possibilities, and be willing to be surprised.

Driving the Bus, Letting Go, and Allowing

As I mentioned previously, I had lived my entire life to this point, trying to control everything. This is what I want, this is what it looks like, and I want this now. That's what I thought manifesting your destiny was all about. I read all the books and watched the videos! I was determined to make things happen, my way.

Since that plan didn't work out so well, perhaps a different approach was necessary. From the moment I stopped trying to force things to happen and started trusting that everything is perfectly created for me, it became easier to adopt a no-worries attitude. This change did not happen overnight, and I admit that my ego still struggles with this new attitude at times. The ego takes its job very seriously, but it's not the ego's job to know why or how or when our desires are going to manifest.

It's important to be clear about what you want, but just consciously repeating what you want over and over will probably not make that thing just suddenly show up in front of you. Although, it could happen. Anything is possible. The next step is getting yourself into a state of inner calmness and stepping into the picture to feel what it will feel like to have that life. This action will put you on the frequency to attract that which you desire or something better. See what you'll be doing, who you'll be with, and what you will have. Really get into the feeling of being and having what you desire. Then, release the vision into the quantum field to be carried out by your higher mind, and trust that your future will unfold in a way that is perfect for you. Bring your awareness back to the present moment. A phrase I use is, "I put this situation in the hands of infinite love and wisdom. I trust in the divine plan," and I let it go.

There is no need to keep asking for the same thing day after day. It would be like telling the waiter at the restaurant what you want to order from the menu, then telling him or her again every five minutes in case he or she didn't hear you the first time. You give the waiter your order once, and you let it go. You return to your conversation with your friends. You return to the moment, and you trust that the waiter will bring you your meal at the right time.

Get out of your own way by remaining open to new opportunities and possibilities. If you cling so tightly to what you believe should be, when the real truth comes knocking, you won't even open the door. Do not get so attached to your vision and to what it should look like, and when it should arrive. By doing that, you are limiting the ways in which your desire can manifest. You might miss wonderful opportunities because something or someone didn't look like what you envisioned. Let it go and trust that your desire will be fulfilled at the perfect time. Do not analyze or try to figure out how, or when, or where it is going to happen; leave those details to a mind that knows so much more than your physical mind does, the part of you that sees the whole picture.

Won't you be surprised when your desire comes in a way that you least expect? It will most likely look even better than what you had imagined. It's so much more exciting this way. To quote American mythologist, Joseph Campbell, "[w]e must be willing to get rid of the life we've planned, so as to have the life that is waiting for us."[7] The physical mind is not the place where ideas are born. That happens in the consciousness of the higher mind in the quantum field. The higher mind conceives the idea, the physical brain receives the information, and the physical mind perceives it. Once you've told the bus driver where you want to go, sit back, and enjoy the ride. Stop trying to drive the bus. It's not your job. Do what you were designed to do. Your job is to experience the journey by responding and reacting to what you perceive. The driver has the big picture map, he or she knows where you want to go and how to get there, so trust him or her. You don't have to know all the details; you don't have to know how or when you're going to get there, just enjoy the experience. It's not urgent that you get there; trust that you are exactly where you're supposed to be. When you take a trip and have a destination in mind, you can't see your destination from where you are, but you trust that you will get there. Whether you're traveling by car, bus, boat, train, or plane, sit back and enjoy the ride, enjoy the view, and enjoy the conversation. You might just see, hear, or say something meaningful in that moment.

Enjoy the mystery. Let life unfold without trying so hard to figure it all out. Simply allow because everything is going to happen in divine order. Just jump into the vortex with both feet, and let the universe do its job!

You think you're in charge of your life, but you're not. The infinite intelligence that is in everything and in everyone, which puts you through all these experiences, is handling everything. All the power

7   https://www.jcf.org/works/quote/we-must-be-willing/

and knowledge you have come from that consciousness. This greater and wiser self must have a loving purpose for all of your experiences. This self knows the end before the beginning. A parenthesis opens up when you are born in this physical realm and closes at the end of your life, and everything in between is handled for you. (Prelife planning will be discussed in chapter 9.)

As human beings, we have trouble trusting what we don't understand, but during the nine-month period before we came into this life, didn't we trust completely in the intelligence that created us? We did, until the ego showed up and said, "I'm in control now. I'll take over from here." We edged God out. So began our struggle to let go and live in the moment.

It took me several years to learn to let go. In everything I do now, I set my intention that this is going to be a fantastic day, that I will meet interesting people, that my meeting will be a great one, and I return to the present moment and allow life to unfold. If meeting this person or getting this new job is in my divine plan, I welcome the opportunity, but if this experience is not meant for me at this time, I give thanks and let this desire go. It's so much easier to flow with the river than against it. The words of this traditional nursery rhyme are a great reminder to:

"[r]ow, row, row your boat,
Gently down the stream.
Merrily, merrily, merrily, merrily,
Life is but a dream.

Let go of your demands and your beliefs that you need this or that to be happy. What is meant to be will find its way to you. If something doesn't turn out the way you wanted, it's a blessing in disguise. Practice allowing that something to be the way it is. Everything you need will be provided for you. The right person, offer, or opportunity will show up at the perfect time. And won't you be pleasantly surprised to have it happen at just the right time for you?

It's not always obvious at the time, but every situation we go through usually makes sense once all the pieces are in place. When we get out of the way and trust, opportunities happen. The perfect solution is already there, and everything we need will appear at exactly the right moment. Some people may call it luck. I like the acronym for LUCK that Michael Beckwith mentioned in one of his lectures, **Living Under Cosmic Knowledge**. When we stop trying to do it alone and surrender our heart and desire to the infinite intelligence, we open the door for the perfect manifestation of that desire. Be in peaceful harmony with that force that has always handled everything. Surrendering does not mean giving up. It means letting go, detaching from the outcome, enjoying the journey while allowing the synchronicity of events to unfold. You are surrendering to the source that created you. Trust in this wisdom to guide you. It knows all your human desires and regrets—no need to push and struggle. It knows the best timing for what you want, and it wants you to know that all will come at the right moment. There's desiring and then there's allowing. You may desire a tomato from your garden, but you must allow the tomato to grow.

Levels of Consciousness

Our conscious mind thinks it's in control, but it represents only five percent of consciousness. Ninety-five percent of our behavior is unconscious.

In describing levels of consciousness, the subconscious and unconscious are sometimes used to describe the same thing. In my hypnotherapy training, the levels of the mind were referred to as the conscious mind, the subconscious mind, the unconscious mind, and the superconscious/higher mind. The subconscious and unconsciousness have slightly different functions.

Level of the mind	Definition
Conscious mind	The action part of the mind, the decider, the part that perceives, judges, rationalizes, decides, and analyzes. It is the mortal mind, the intellect, and it thinks it rules the world. You can compare it to the captain of a ship or the king of a kingdom who makes decisions on how to administer his kingdom. It is the home of the ego, the personality.
Subconscious mind	The part of the mind that produces imagery that is readily available to the conscious mind. The king's faithful servant, a silent listener. Located just below the awareness of ordinary consciousness, its purpose is to obey without analysis, to fulfill the captain's orders or wishes of the king. It does not have a sense of humor; it simply does what it is directed to do. It is more powerful than the conscious mind that thinks it makes the rules. In other words, it is your genie in the bottle, waiting to fulfill your wishes. It is always ready to deliver the orders it has been given.

Unconscious mind	The area of the mind that produces imagery that is generally unavailable to the conscious mind. It contains forgotten information. It is the storehouse of all experiences, thoughts, and feelings. It registers everything we see and hear. Our unconscious keeps track of millions of bits of information simultaneously. Our conscious mind can process only forty bits of information per second. Most people can think of about seven things all at once; we can think of the sound of someone's voice, the music playing in the background, how our hair looks, what the other person's attire looks like, how tired our feet might be from standing there while we're talking to our friend, what we're going to say next, how warm we feel, but not much beyond that. Our unconscious mind keeps track of everything else for us. If we had to consciously think about each breath we take or about each step we take, it would be impossible to function throughout the day. Most of us have experienced what is called the driving trance, where our mind can wander wherever, thinking about anything at all, while our feet and hands know exactly what to do as we move through traffic. If we had to think about each movement our feet and hands had to take, it would be very difficult to get where we want to go.

Superconscious/ higher mind	The part of the mind that connects oneself to everything else and represents mass consciousness and spiritual and intuitive insights. The area that gives us intuition or information about other people, places, and things. It is also referred to as the God or divine mind within each person. It knows the full blueprint of every life experience.

In summary, the conscious mind sets the course, so the individual knows where he or she wants to go. The subconscious mind provides the imagery needed to fulfill the person's wishes. The unconscious mind brings forgotten thoughts and feelings to awareness, so the person can achieve his or her goal, and it provides resources and insights. The superconscious/higher mind adds an important dimension. It gives intuitive and spiritual insight from the nonphysical dimensions of thought. At this level, mind-body-spirit are one. The superconscious information travels through the unconscious to the subconscious and then to the conscious mind. What we hear, see, touch, smell, and taste are electrical signals interpreted by our brain. Once our brain interprets the information, it is perceived as reality. Reality is one hundred percent subjective because it is based on our personal experience of our brain. As Albert Einstein was known to say about our minds: "[T]he intuitive mind is a sacred gift, and the rational mind is a faithful servant. We have created a society that honors the servant and has forgotten the gift."-[8]

---

8 http://quotesjournal.blogspot.com/2020/08/the-intuitive-mind-is-sacred-gift-and.html

Fear Gets in the Way

We are quick to blame other people or situations for what happens or doesn't happen to us. We can blame our parents, religion, God, the government, or the weather, but as long as we hold on to blaming, we stop ourselves from being free. We have assigned power to something outside of ourselves and have created obstacles that prevent us from living our greatest life.

No one is responsible for how you feel. If you think that what someone did or said to you caused you to feel hurt, insulted, angry, or sad, think again. That person was put on your path to help you see what you're still holding onto, what you are still giving power to. There is no need to blame your parents or anyone who abused you in your life, including yourself. It's time to stop the abuse, to free yourself from letting the ego control your life.

There is a higher consciousness directing this movie, and all you have to do is choose how you're going to react to the scenes. Every actor is playing his or her role, and everyone agreed to this. They are reading their scripts and you are reading yours.

I am reminded of the first lines of William Shakespeare's "All the World's a Stage" poem:

> All the world's a stage,
> And all the men and women merely players;
> They have their exits and their entrances;
> And one man in his time plays many parts.[9]

For example, when you're watching a movie and a situation moves you, you don't blame the actor or the director for your feelings. You don't ask the actor to play his part differently so you'll feel better. You may recall watching a movie or television series and how you easily became attached to and involved with the characters and the events

---

9   https://en.wikipedia.org/wiki/All_the_world%27s_a_stage

in their lives, and then how sad and upset you were when the main character died. Then you realize that it's just a movie; it's not real.

People in your own life movie are not the cause of your pain or discomfort, and they are not going to change their behavior to make you feel better. Only you are responsible for your reaction to what you observe. Who or what shows up in your life is just an opportunity for you to be aware of feelings you are still holding on to. No one has to change so you'll feel better or be happier. Take one hundred percent responsibility for how you feel, and change your reaction. When I first came to this realization, I faced extreme inner resistance. I absolutely did not want to accept that I was responsible for my feelings. How was that possible? It was so much easier to play the victim and blame someone else for making me feel sad or hurt. It took me over forty years to realize and acknowledge that if someone's behavior determines your happiness or lack of it, you are attached to that person. You have given your power to that person. The source of that attachment is fear. It took two marriages for me to figure that one out.

Fear is the first emotion we feel as babies, and it is the basis of all the judgments, beliefs, and opinions that we develop. We might experience fear the first time we become aware that our mother has left us alone in the crib and has left the room. We cry, no one is there. We feel abandoned. It could be a time when we first hear our parents arguing or talking in loud voices. I can't say that ever happened in our house when I was growing up. I never heard my parents arguing about anything, not once. Maybe it happened in your household. Hearing a loud argument can be scary to a baby, who cannot make sense of his or her environment but can sense the energy in the room.

Such moments can create fear in a baby. Most of those early moments are not remembered at the conscious level, but depending on the emotional effect they had, they can be buried deep in our unconscious mind. In early childhood, we operate mostly at the subconscious level. We don't understand and process experiences. The subconscious doesn't analyze anything; it just takes in all the information, and each time a similar situation appears, it plays back everything that was recorded and filed in the unconscious mind.

I remember times when I was afraid as a child. My earliest impactful, fearful memory originates from when I was about two-and-a-half or three years old. We lived on a farm, and one morning, there were a couple of bear cubs stuck in a tree not far from our house. They didn't know how to get down on their own, so our mother decided to go and see if she could help them get down from that tree. My brother, who is a just a few years older than me, was sitting beside me on top of a table by the window as we watched our mother walk toward the bears. I had heard my older brothers and sisters talk about when you see baby bears, it means that their mama is usually not too far behind. So, what do you think was going through my mind at that moment? Mama bear is going to show up and attack my mom. I remember that both my brother and I were crying, thinking that mama bear was going to kill our mother. It turned out that mama bear was nowhere to be found; she had most likely been killed by hunters, and her cubs were on their own. So, the good news was that our mother was not eaten by a bear that day, but the emotion attached to the fear I experienced had been well recorded in my subconscious mind. The fear of losing someone you love, the person who takes care of you, and for me, the fear of being abandoned were implanted in my subconscious that day.

Another memory that follows along the same trail of fearful emotion was my first day in kindergarten at the age of four. I was very afraid of being left in the classroom with strangers. I hadn't been among people other than my family. I didn't want my mother to leave me. I know I'm not the only one this has happened to. I witnessed similar behavior in some of the children in my years as a kindergarten teacher. Again, at the moment that my mother left me in the kindergarten, I experienced the fearful emotion of abandonment, which was recorded in my subconscious.

Then there's the memory of the first time my parents went on a trip to another city. They had never left me before, and it seemed as though they were going so far away that I might never see them again. I remember the sensation of being afraid that they were leaving me. By then, I had already formed a judgment that I would lose someone I love from previous similar events, which turned into a belief that they were abandoning me. I had formed an opinion based on that fear.

We also acquire fears from our parents or siblings by observing their reactions, their behaviors, or their words. From those fearful experiences, we form judgments, resistances that then become beliefs, and we form opinions according to the beliefs. The opinions are then carried through our entire life and called upon automatically. Until we stop and realize that the story of this movie is based on conclusions we came to during early childhood experiences, this belief continues to be the frame of reference guiding our life. The same patterns keep showing up, and we keep wondering why. As a friend of mine remarked one day during a conversation about this subject, "the people are wearing different disguises but the pattern, the feeling, is exactly the same as those previous situations."

Looking back, I realize that the fear of being abandoned played a major role in both my marriages. This truth was right there in front of me the whole time, but I was resisting it. The ego can have such a strong hold on us that we can miss the message that is staring us in the face. The fear can be buried so deeply that all we can see is what our ego is showing us and telling us, the story it has created for us.

I stayed in my first marriage for a few years longer than I would have liked because I was afraid of not knowing who was going to take care of me if I left. That seemed more important than my happiness. I'm probably not the only who has ever been or will be in a similar situation. I was afraid that if I did what I really wanted to that I would be abandoned. I was also afraid of being judged—what would my family and friends think of me—and I created an entire scenario in my mind. Other people's expectations of me had a huge influence in my life. More beliefs from my religious upbringing also added to the script of this story, and that little voice kept telling me that I could not break the vow of marriage I had taken. Old recordings would start to play, "when you get married, it's for life. You stay together no matter what." I was so overwhelmed by all these old, fear-based beliefs that I wasn't even aware of what was happening. I did not recognize the obvious pattern. I wasn't ready to see it. I reacted the only way I knew at that moment.

After six or seven years of having that conversation with my ego, I finally got the courage to leave, and I jumped right into the arms of the man who came to rescue me. Yes, the one who had just about knocked me off my stool when he mysteriously showed up to join my meditation class. I literally left my house and moved in overnight with that man who later became my second husband, and you guessed it, the same pattern continued. The ideal candidate was put on my path to show me what beliefs I was still holding on to. He played his role perfectly, even though I didn't see it at the time. The universe really has a great sense of humor. It's quite hilarious when you think about it. The man was everything I wanted in a partner. He was tall, dark, and handsome. He was intelligent with a great sense of humor, and we were on similar spiritual paths. At that level, we totally understood each other. It was magical. The universe was our playground. Even when I was writing this chapter of my book, I received a social media message from him, saying that in the past few days or weeks, he had seen three license plates while in traffic with the letters GRZ on them, the first three letters of my last name. When we were together, we often received messages or signs from the universe this way, validating something we happened to be working on. Our friends used to say we were a match made in heaven! We were indeed, although not the way I had planned it.

Heaven had a perfect plan, but it didn't look like mine; so, I didn't recognize it at the time.

The fear of being abandoned and my attempt to control the situation so I wouldn't be abandoned still waited for my notice, and that man was the perfect candidate. It was so easy for me to get attached to this person because he looked exactly like the man I wanted. I was instantly attracted to him—physically, mentally, and spiritually. The universe had sent me the perfect package, and I became totally attached to this man. My happiness depended on him, and I either felt happy or sad, according to the way he behaved. I tried to get him to act the way I thought was the perfect way. I wanted to control his behavior instead of allowing him to be who he was. If I wasn't with him one hundred percent of the time, I became uncontrollably sad and worried of being left alone. As I mentioned earlier, if someone's behavior determines your happiness or lack of it, you are attached to that person.

He came into my life to play his role, which I know was an agreement we had made on a deeper level as all interactions with other people are agreements. From our spiritual work during our eight years together, we quickly became aware that we had a connection that transcended space and time. He read his script as agreed, so I would see what I was still holding on to. I resisted acknowledging that at the time because I was so focused on what I wanted our relationship to be like. The ego persisted in having me hold on to that familiar belief, which was all based on fear. I refused to see that the more I tried to control him, the more pain I experienced. He became very resentful and unkind, which is a normal reaction whenever someone tries to control us. I held on to him so tight that he lost his freedom to fly, but I sure couldn't see that at the time.

This applies not only to our personal relationships but to any relationships, whether with a coworker or someone who crosses our path for a brief moment. Don't blame the actors for your feelings, blaming will continue to hold you back. In the words of the following Chinese proverb, "[h]e who blames others has a long way to go on his journey. He who blames himself is halfway there. He who blames no one has arrived."[10] Be grateful that the actors show up when you need them most so that you continue to peel away the layers of the ego, and you will have arrived. Trying to control everything and everyone for fear of being abandoned was exposed in my first marriage where I was controlled and in my second marriage where I became the controller. Then, after I lost everything, I realized that I'm not the one in control. I am grateful that these shadows were exposed, and I no longer blame myself or the actors, who played their roles perfectly.

---

10 https://www.goodreads.com/quotes/9993888-he-who-blames-others-has-a-long-way-to-go

CHAPTER 5

THE EGO / THE PERSONALITY

"As soon as you are born you are given a name, a
religion, a nationality, and a race. You spend the
rest of your life defending a fictional identity."

— Author unknown

The ego does not have to control your life. You are not your ego.
It looks and feels real, but it's not; it's part of the human story. It
is simply a mask you wear while playing a role, but you are not the
mask. The ego has you convinced that you are what you have, what
you do, and that you are your reputation or what others think of
you. The ego and its beliefs want you to think it's real. It does such
a great job at keeping your mind busy and distracted with all the
drama; it has you believing this is who you really are. The ego sur-
vives on emotions created by fear. Remember, beliefs are just stories
that keep the ego alive.

The entire system we live in is ruled by fear, a perfect playground
for the ego. Governments say, obey, or you will go to jail; schools say,
obey, or you will fail; religions say, obey, or you will go to hell.

How many limiting beliefs come from the religion we grew up with or the society we grew up in? I've often heard people say, "I can't do this because it goes against my beliefs or my religion." Every culture has created its own stories, based on similar misconceptions, and because religion says something is so, we decide it must be a fact. We were taught to not ask questions, "just take our word for it; we will tell you what it all means. You have to go through us to find the answers." We start to believe that we can't access this divine guidance on our own, that we must get it from authority figures. So, we wonder, "who am I to talk to God?"

From the time humans started asking questions that no one could answer, we were told, "we don't know if it's possible to know," which eventually became "we don't have a need to know," which then turned into a religious and political doctrine of "we are not supposed to know."

Some religious teachings would have us believe that we are sinners—unworthy, guilty—and that we should ask for forgiveness because we have done something wrong. From the time we are very young, we are taught that God is vengeful and that we will be punished for our sins and go to hell. That is all very upsetting and frightening to a child. It was to me. I remember being very afraid of the way the angels on the church ceiling looked down on me. From the looks on their faces, I was convinced that I must have done something terribly wrong, and God was going to punish me. Instead of feeling loved by the angels, I felt anxious and scared. When you add to those feelings the story of Adam and Eve in the Garden of Eden, it leaves one feeling unworthy. Eve, seduced by the serpent, tempted Adam with the fruit of the Tree of Knowledge of Good and Evil, which, after they ate it, made them realize that they were naked, and an angry God banished them from paradise because they committed a sin; this tale all plays along quite well with the ego's game, designed to control—to create doubt and fear. Eating from the Tree of Knowledge of Good and Evil was the beginning of judgment for our race. Not only did Adam and Eve judge that being naked was something to be ashamed of, they also judged that they had done something wrong. The Tree of Knowledge of Good and Evil is just another name for the Tree of Judgment.

We believe that because the first man and woman were bad, we are all declared imperfect the moment we are born in to this world and that all sense of perfection ended when the original sin was committed. This belief is a trap, a control mechanism. That little voice has been whispering in your ear, "you've been bad; you have disobeyed; you have committed a sin; you are not worthy; you should be ashamed; you don't deserve to be happy" for quite a while. Such stories have been repeated over many generations, and we have grown up believing that they must be true; we are imperfect in the eyes of God. We have been on a quest for perfection ever since, trying to change ourselves and others because we assume that there's something wrong with us. Evidence of this requirement to be perfect can be found in the stories of other cultures as well.

This is just a belief—it's not the real you, not your identity; it's just the personality you created along the way. Within the first few months of your life, you lived in this realm of unity with everything; you were aware of the one infinite reality. As you explored your new environment through your five senses, you began to react to other people's behaviors and events around you, and sometimes you were traumatized. Each time something happened, it became part of your story and your personality developed. Increasingly, you started to identify with this personality, and your relationship with your true essence faded. You eventually lost sight of the real you and started to experience life through the filter of the ego, which, by then, had you convinced that you were separate, an individual living in a physical body in a material world. The ego wants you to believe that who you are is what you do, what you have, and what others think of you. This personality has worked diligently from that time to maintain the illusion. Deep within, we all know this is an illusion, but our egos have done a great job of convincing us otherwise.

You picked up much baggage from your surroundings, parents, siblings, friends, teachers, and church, and you formed judgments and beliefs from the time you showed up in this life experience. This personality, the ego, wants you to feel bad, sad, and guilty because that's what keeps it alive. It thrives on drama and suffering. It wants you to believe that holding on to that negative feeling is beneficial, that you're getting something out of it. Drama is the result of what you believe.

Since we believe that God judges us, we believe that it is okay to judge others. Not only do we judge others, but we judge and punish ourselves endlessly. If we make a mistake, we feel guilty, bad, or unworthy. We become addicted to the beliefs of self-pity, jealousy, guilt, or anger. We get hooked on the familiar recording that keeps playing in our mind, "I'm not pretty enough, smart enough, good enough... I'm not worthy... or, What will they think of me?..." Realize that when you question your worthiness, you are saying that the supreme intelligence that created you doesn't know what it's doing. Creation doesn't make mistakes. You are perfect, and so is everyone else. Why not cancel the subscription to all the beliefs that you carry around with you?

This belief system all began with fear, and it prevents us from being who we really are. It's not in alignment with our true identity. We pick up beliefs from our environment because we think we need to be a certain way to fit in or to behave a certain way to get along. We become very emotionally attached to our beliefs because we have invested many years in them, and we depend on them to lead our lives. As Dr. Wayne Dyer puts it, "[a] belief system is nothing more than a thought you've thought over and over again."[11] From this, we can see that we might have a lot invested in our belief systems, but those beliefs don't need to make us who we are. Indeed, we carry

11 https://www.drwaynedyer.com/?s=belief

beliefs around that are not even ours; they don't belong to us. Beliefs come from outside of us. Know the difference between a belief and a knowing. A knowing comes from within; it is beyond the physical. If a belief weighs you down, it's a sign that it's not yours. A knowing will never let you down. It's time to give back the beliefs that don't belong to you. What belongs to you is uplifting and exciting.

We want to be loved and accepted by others; in the words of Rumi, "I want to sing like the birds sing, not worrying about who hears or what they think."[12] But we have a difficult time accepting and loving ourselves. Our real identities get pushed aside. Let go of the fear that you aren't pretty enough, smart enough, or good enough. It's time to free yourself from these shackles.

No Right and Wrong—Letting Go of Judgment

You see, there were two trees in the Garden of Eden, the Tree of Good and Evil, where all judgment began, and the Tree of Life. Man did not experience that tree because he was apparently driven out of the garden before that happened. So, Adam and Eve ate of the Tree of Illusion and saw the illusion of good and evil, right and wrong (false powers that man created for himself), instead of the one power, God. In the Garden of Eden, the mind of man initially functioned at the superconscious level, where whatever he desired or required was always available. With the Tree of Illusion came the development of the reasoning mind, and man reasoned himself into the illusion of lack, limitations, and failure. Don't despair; there is hope. From the Book of Revelation, "[t]o him that overcometh will I give to eat of the Tree of Life, which is in the midst of the paradise of God."[13] This book reveals to us that good and evil are judgments and that the battle is not about the end of the world, but about letting go of judgments. Let go of judgments, and experience the Tree of Life.

---

12 https://wisdomquotes.com/rumi-quotes/
13 https://biblehub.com/asv/revelation/2.htm

Your infinite self is the Tree of Life within you, your source. To quote Rumi, "[o]ut beyond ideas of wrongdoing and rightdoing, there is a field. I will meet you there."[14]

You have never done anything wrong; every experience is valuable. Stop believing the ego. Everything that happens is a gift, an opportunity to know yourself. We may not know how a situation serves us at the moment it occurs, and there is no need to try to figure out what it means. That event or situation is there to show us what is still weighing us down.

Our own judgment and resistance toward ourselves, someone else, or something causes our pain, suffering, and stress. Even though we can't control someone or a situation, we can control how we react to that situation or person. Instead of judging a situation as good or bad, develop an awareness and acceptance that feelings are neither good nor bad because who knows what's good or bad?

The beliefs that were born from judgments are what keep the story alive. Beliefs stored in our minds are just that, beliefs that are ruled by fear. It's all made-up, it's not real. Beliefs justify the ego's existence. If the ego thinks that you are trying to get rid of it, it will do everything it can to defend itself; it will fight you all the way and continue to become stronger. When it feels ignored, it will try to force its presence into your conscious thoughts and behavior.

When we stop listening to the ego about how things should or shouldn't be and release all judgments, we find just what is. That's why it's a good idea to have, what I call, a *BS detector*. Don't believe everything your ego tells you. Whatever is filtered by the ego is distorted. If you allow doubt and anxiety to rule your decisions, those decisions will lead only to disappointment. Remind yourself that the source of that story is usually based on fear. When doubt comes up, say, "thank-you for sharing," and don't hold on to the story.

Beliefs are stories. We need stories to justify our feelings of guilt or pain from past situations. The ego wants us to attach meaning

14 https://wisdomquotes.com/rumi-quotes/

to the story. These beliefs weigh us down and keep us in the past, playing the same recording repeatedly, an endless repetition of self-importance. Remember, the ego doesn't want you to change the stories; it's trying to maintain its existence, and giving up the story, the illusion, would mean the end of something.

If we want to be free, we must let go and trust that everything is exactly as it should be. There have been times when I looked back at my two marriages that I thought of myself as having failed at being married. The expression *failed marriage*, which we often hear, came to mind. You know, just because a story has ended, it doesn't mean it was a failure. That's just another belief, and, yes, it was just a story. The story of your life has many chapters, and it's okay to close a chapter and begin a new one, or you can even put a book aside and begin a new one. What happened no longer matters; it has ceased to be. That moment no longer exists; there is only now.

Beliefs cannot deactivate themselves. As long as the judgment remains, the belief remains. As long as we judge and resist a situation, we stay in that experience. The more we resist something and try to run away from it, the more it will run after us. When we stop judging, we stop giving power to that person or situation, we stop playing the game of the ego. Once we eliminate the judgment, we end the story. Without judgment, every scene in your movie is perfect. If there is no judgment, there is no need for a belief, so it ceases to exist, and you break free from the shackles.

Our ego not only creates stories about our past situations, it also creates stories to justify our future anxieties or to explain how something will happen. Since what our physical mind perceives is limited by our beliefs, this situation creates more limitations. If we think we know better and we know exactly how this thing we want should come about, aren't we perhaps preventing all other unimagined possibilities to manifest? Requiring a story creates much limitation. It determines the range of what you can receive. Our limited beliefs and thoughts limit the possibilities of how we can receive what we desire. This limitation applies to everything we want, whether it's a relationship, a career, or money. Keep an open mind and heart. The possibilities are limitless, so why put walls around them?

Reciting positive affirmations all day long won't help us achieve our goal if deep down we continue to hold on to the story. Such enumeration will not change anything. Positive affirmations are wonderful, but they are just an intellectual exercise, and if at a deeper level we are still resisting something because of a judgment or belief, we will continue to have more of the same. We see only what we believe is possible. Trying to focus on positive thoughts simply means that we are resisting negative ones. In the words of Michael Beckwith, "[a]ffirmations don't make something happen, they make something welcome."[15] This exercise opens the door, but you have to get rid of the clutter to achieve a deeper knowing. Your feelings will guide you within.

Forgiveness Is about Understanding

Forgiveness is a topic that we hear and read much about in our search for self-improvement. You have probably come across phrases such as, *"You must forgive yourself and others if you want to move on"* or, *"Forgiveness is the key."* Holding on to such a belief could slow down your spiritual growth. In this sense, forgiveness conforms with other concepts created by religions, made-up to fulfill God's conditional requirements, condoning the *bad* things that you have done or that were done to you.

Let's think outside that box for a moment. What if there is nothing to forgive? Contemplate that. If you think you need to forgive someone for something that they did to you or to someone else, wouldn't that imply that you believe that he or she did something wrong? Wouldn't you still be judging that person or their behavior? Which takes you right back to the same old beliefs, and you continue to play the game of the ego. You see how that works? This is another belief designed to keep you in the game, therefore, hindering your spiritual growth.

---

15 https://www.azquotes.com/quote/839825

When there is understanding, there is no need for forgiveness. When someone has done something that made you feel mad or angry or disappointed, ask yourself if you have ever behaved in the same way. When you put yourself in the other person's shoes, you will most likely realize that you have done something similar to someone else, perhaps when you were going through a tough time, and took out your frustration on another person. When you elevate your consciousness to that level, you understand that there is nothing to forgive. We can take this to a deeper level, but I will leave that discussion for later. Understanding brings peace. You no longer let an outdated belief be an obstacle that stands in the way of living your best life in the present.

It's your choice; you can stay in the game or break free. As previously stated, when we stop judging, we stop playing the game of the ego. It ceases to exist. When you eliminate judgment, you end the story. Without judgment, everything is perfect. Let go of judgments, and experience the Tree of Life.

It doesn't matter what the other person's agenda is. Other people's drama does not belong to you and is not yours to judge. There is an old Polish proverb that goes like this: "Not my circus. Not my monkeys."[16] It's a great line to remember, it works quite well as a reminder. I use it often.

It's not about forgiving yourself either because that would mean that you judge yourself for having done something wrong. Maybe forgiving could be replaced with comforting. Just like your hand does not need to forgive your toe for stubbing itself, but your hand could comfort your toe instead. If you feel bad about something you did in the past that you think you need to forgive yourself for, how about understanding and comforting yourself instead. You have never done anything wrong. Stop believing the ego. Every experience is perfect and valuable.

---

16 https://en.wiktionary.org/wiki/not_my_circus,_not_my_monkeys

Choosing to Let Go of the Ego

Once you tell the truth about a situation, the truth being that no one or nothing is responsible for how you feel, you are one step closer to letting go of the ego and reclaiming your power. Taking responsibility plus being aware equal power. Instead of asking why something is happening to you or why this person did something to you, start paying attention to your reaction and the feelings that come up. Only then will you get closer to being happy and start enjoying the ride.

Happiness is a choice. Your own mind is the cause of happiness as well as the cause of suffering. You hold tight to your stories; you believe them, defend them, and give them much importance. You have the power to react to what happens in your movie. You also have the power to exit the movie theater entirely. It's your choice. As illustrated in *Plato's Allegory of the Cave*, we are like prisoners in a cave, who only see what is projected on the screen in front of us. We have become so emotionally attached to the scenes and characters in our movie that it has become our reality. We believe what we see is real. Movies are designed to make us believe what we see on the screen to be real, even though we know what we are watching is a false reality. When someone walks out of the cave or the movie theater, and is awakened to a whole new reality, that person wants to return to the cave to tell others of his discovery. The people in the cave cannot understand his stories, and the thought of leaving the cave is much too scary. They prefer to continue watching the shadows on the wall. The lack of understanding of this person's stories does not make the stories any less real. We can step out beyond the confines of the theater at any time, and become enlightened to other realities.

Physical reality is an illusion, an experience in consciousness. It is not about escaping the illusion; it's about being liberated of its ability to control your reality while living with it. The illusion is intended to be a tool you can use to enjoy this reality; it provides a context within which you can experience the many aspects of yourself. Becoming a master of this illusion doesn't mean that you change it; you change your perception of it. It means that, regardless of what's going on, you remain in a blissful state, free of the illusion's ability to control you. Beliefs can be manipulated and changed. You can choose to believe that the shadows are all there is or that there exists another reality beyond this one. We once believed in a reality that the earth was flat and that the sun revolved around the earth! You never change anyone or anything. Change your beliefs, and you change your perception of reality. Your personality creates your personal reality, and your reality can be a beautiful dream or a nightmare.

Focus on yourself, live a life free of conflict with yourself and with others. Live a life without fear, and that's what will be reflected back to you. How you perceive the world is a reflection of your state of consciousness. If you see the world through the filter of people can't be trusted, you will see evidence that supports that belief all around you. If you view the world through the filter of people are kind and loving, that's what you will draw to yourself. Heaven and hell are not places. They are states of being, right here, right now. You are walking and living in one of them on this earth. You experience heaven when you are one with all that is, when you know your true self. You experience hell when you separate yourself from that source; you try to find yourself, but it seems impossible to be reunited.

You are living your perception of reality, and how you choose to respond or react to the world around you determines your reality. Leave the cave and find out who you really are.

You can continue to let the ego control you, or you can reclaim your power now and experience heaven on earth. In the words of Dr. Wayne Dyer, "[y]ou can either be a Host to God, or a Hostage to your ego!"[17] Ancients texts all point to the fact that to be free we must let go of our habits of judging and criticizing. The

17 https://www.drwaynedyer.com/

crucifixion symbolizes the voluntary relinquishment of the ego when the soul returns to God. The kingdom of heaven is without hate and judgment.

Do what's right for you. If something resonates with you, explore that. If something is not serving you, let it go. Before doing something, ask yourself if it will bring you total joy and total happiness to do it. If not, let it go; walk away; get rid of it. You will naturally distance yourself from who and what no longer serves you. To quote Albert Einstein, "[s]tay away from negative people. They have a problem for every solution."[18] I have met people like that, and I have walked away. You can still be kind to toxic people, but distance yourself quickly, and let life be their teacher. I have and continue to let go of what no longer serves me. It's their circus, their monkeys. I choose to be happy and to surround myself with people who inspire me. It's perfectly okay to be happy and to express your joy. There's enough happiness to go around. Your being happy will not prevent someone else from being happy. So, be happy.

Looking at life through the ego is like looking through a periscope—an instrument for observation over, around, or through an object, obstacle, or condition that prevents direct line-of-sight observation from an observer's current position. This can be fun and interesting for a while, but it allows you to see only a tiny piece of the picture. Only when you can see past the filters of the ego personality, can you be aware of the bigger picture and experience your real self.

---

18 https://wisdomquotes.com/albert-einstein-quotes/

CHAPTER 6

LOOK IN THE MIRROR

It's so much easier to look to the outside for how you feel, to blame someone or something out there because looking inside means taking responsibility and getting past the ego. If you want to experience the Tree of Life and be free, go ahead, look inside, look in the mirror. Other people are the mirror. They are playing their role to reflect back to you what you need to see. Be grateful.

The quantum mind is like a big mirror; it reflects back to you what you accept and believe as true. If you feel that you are not loved, it is a projection of your own reluctance to love yourself. If you feel like you don't receive the recognition you deserve, it is a projection of you not giving enough recognition to yourself. These reflections started at some point in your life story, and most of these feelings were not even yours to begin with; they belonged to someone else. From the moment we begin to form in our mother's womb, we begin to sense the emotions of our mother. We can sense when she is sad, depressed, or upset, and these feelings get imprinted on our subconscious mind—only to remain there as part of our personality until they are acknowledged and transformed. This is a situation I frequently came across with clients in my hypnotherapy practice. When directed to go to the moment that a particular feeling began, individuals would find themselves in the warm, peaceful environment of their mother's womb and clearly aware of their mother's feelings. Once they understood the source of the sadness or upset, they could decide to let the emotion go.

From the time I can remember, sadness was a recurring theme in my life, and I spent many years trying to figure out where that sadness came from. I have always been a naturally happy person, but occasionally, I would experience an intense sadness that was associated with the feeling of not being loved, but I didn't understand it. From my perception growing up, my mother seemed to carry some sadness deep within. I don't know her story; she never talked about it, but she seemed emotionally absent and rarely expressed her love, at least not in the way I would have liked. I sensed my mother's sadness from the time I was just a few years old. As a young child, I interpreted that feeling and formed an opinion that I must have done something wrong, and that's why she was sad. Her actions, or lack of them, supported that belief. She never took me in her arms and hugged me and never said she loved me. I thought she didn't love me, which led me to believe that I must be unlovable. By accepting that belief as true, people showed up in my life to reflect it back to me. My first husband was emotionally absent, and my second husband didn't love me the way I would have liked. I continued to have moments of unexplainable deep-seated sadness.

If you still have unfinished business with your parents, teachers, or siblings, these emotions will be reflected back to you from the people in your life right here, right now. Since everyone is a mirror, they reflect back to you what you need to see. We can sometimes search for answers for many years, and fail to see the answer because we are resisting letting a familiar feeling go. The ego has us convinced that we should hold on to it. When we see what we consider a fault in someone else, instead of judging that person, we can decide immediately to overcome or suppress such fault in our own personality. It will not disappear by just running away from it. Once we look in the mirror and acknowledge what is being reflected back, we are able to transform it.

Your physical reality is just a reflection of what's inside, but just telling yourself that you are happy will not put a smile on your face, not for long anyway. If you look at yourself in the mirror, and you see someone who is sad, depressed, or angry, you can't go to the mirror and make the reflection look happy or peaceful. Once you explore that reflection and the feelings behind it and make the decision to let go of the story, a different reality will be reflected back to you. The mirror has no choice but to reflect back to you what you put out.

From Thinking to Feeling

Some say that life is a school, and we're here to learn lessons. Perhaps life is a school, but for the ego. What if life is just a ride in an amusement park, and it's supposed to be fun? What if our purpose for being here is not just to learn something, but to experience something?

Trying to solve the cause of our pain or suffering by just thinking probably won't get us very far. The ego, disguised as that little voice that does its best to always be in our head, will quickly jump in and convince us that we should hold on to that pain or that guilt, that we deserve to be treated that way. So, we push the rewind and play buttons to replay the situation over and over in our mind, reliving what he or she did and said and how we reacted. That makes us feel even worse, so we jump in and ask, "how could he or she do that to me, or say such things to me, or why is he or she so mean to me?" It's time to stop thinking so much about what the ego wants us to believe and to start feeling, so we can clear the way to enjoy this fun ride our soul wants us to experience. In our feelings, we will find the answers.

Your emotions are your guidance system, but you are not your emotions. Consider the emotions that bring you less than pure joy and excitement to be red flags that lead you to your beliefs and judgments. These emotions are put there so that you can clear them out of your system and become a clear channel of expression for the infinite intelligence. As you experience these emotions, the feeling that comes up will help you trace back the source of the fear that set this trail of events in motion. An *e-motion* is energy in motion. When you are experiencing an irritating situation, choose to remain silent instead of responding verbally, and look inside with curiosity. Be aware of what feeling comes up, and allow it to move however it moves without judging, labeling, or defending it; just notice where it shows up in your body. Just be with what is.

It's preferable to say, "I am experiencing or feeling anger," for example, instead of saying, "I am angry." Then notice where you are experiencing this emotion. Emotions will intensify if you don't acknowledge them. That energy in motion will penetrate the cells of your body and, since it has to find an outlet to express itself, it has the potential of causing an illness. Your mind, body, and spirit are all connected; they work as a team. In the book *Feelings Buried Alive Never Die* by Karol K. Truman, there is a chapter called "Probable Feelings Causing Illness" that I have found to be very useful in identifying the mental, physical, and spiritual connection of an illness. It's a good place to start to open the door to find answers. I still use it often as a reference guide.

It's a good idea to give the emotion a voice, preventing it from expressing itself physically. I have seen this in my own life as well as in my clients' life experiences. If an illness or pain shows up in your life, your body is talking to you. When that happens, ask your inner wisdom what you need to know about the situation. This happened to me on October 1, 2018. I started experiencing acute chest pain that felt like I was having a heart attack. The pain started between my shoulder blades, like I was being stabbed in the back, and came right through to my chest. Then I felt a sharp, shooting pain toward my left shoulder. My entire chest area felt so tight, I could hardly breathe.

After several hours of testing in the emergency room, I was diagnosed with pericarditis, an inflammation of the lining around the heart, which had caused an increase of water around the heart. The cause of pericarditis is often unknown but is usually the result of a serious illness. However, it is more commonly caused by a viral infection. Since the test results indicated that I was in perfect health, the doctor said it was most likely a viral infection.

This incident really got my attention. This condition can be fatal if not treated immediately. What was my body trying to tell me? I, of course, went to the reference section of *Feelings Buried Alive Never Die*, and among some of the feelings associated with heart problems, it states violating the laws of love knowingly or unknowingly, feelings of resentment and/or hurt, not feeling approval from others, and wanting release from responsibility as possibilities. If that wasn't enough validation, and just in case I didn't understand the message, a few days later, I came across an article about the planet Venus going retrograde from October 5 to November 16, 2018. In essence, the article stated that this retrograde represented a time for self-care and self-love, a time to stop bending over backwards for others, and to stop saying yes to everyone and everything.

To further this process, I wrote down my feelings about what I had just read, and it was a perfect match. I was tolerating so much more than was acceptable at work, saying yes to everyone around me, and feeling resentful that I was being paid less than other coworkers. I was making myself sick, bending over backward for others and not caring for myself. I wanted to be released from the overload of responsibilities I had been given, and I was not getting approval from my boss. This had been going on for a few years, and I was allowing it to go on. I was out of alignment with my inner wisdom. I got the message. I started saying no more often, and I asked for a reduction of certain tasks at work. My health had to come first.

Giving your emotions a voice will help you move through your emotions without holding on to them, freeing you to get beyond the ego and into the realm of being, which is the desire of your higher self. Write down what you are feeling, have a nonjudgmental conversation with that pain, that illness, or that guilt, or that sadness. Putting it down on paper lets you detach from it, to look at it from a different perspective, and see it objectively. Sort of like being your own therapist.

The Exercise

Find a place where you can sit quietly, where you will not be disturbed. It's a good idea to have a pen and paper nearby, so you can write down what comes up. You can close your eyes if you wish, and bring the particular situation or person to your mind that *made you feel this way*. This memory should be very easy for you since you have probably replayed this scenario through your mind several times since it happened. Ask yourself, "what am I thinking or feeling right now?" Scan your body for where that feeling is. Give that feeling a voice. As you replay the details of the event, with the dialogue and the actions that took place, start writing down whatever thoughts come to your mind. Without judgment, without analysis, just write whatever comes to you. Your inner wisdom will lead you exactly to what is important for you to see. Once you're done, read what you've written several times—until you discover what negative beliefs and stories are still hidden. Awareness and acknowledgment open the door to allow you to shed those limiting beliefs and to reprogram your subconscious mind with empowering beliefs.

Here is one of my personal examples, "when she talks to me that way, she doesn't value what I say, doesn't care about my opinion; it's as if what I just said was totally useless and that I have to explain and defend what I just said. Makes me feel worthless. She has no respect for me. I don't deserve to be treated that way. She gets defensive and snaps at me, as if I'm blaming her for whatever we were discussing."

Writing down your thoughts and feelings allows you to then step back and see the situation in black and white. The answer will become obvious to you when you are ready to see it. From my example above, I picked up key words such as worthless, respect, deserve, defensive, and blaming.

Once you have written down the details of the situation, you can then further explore the feelings attached to the scenario. Close your eyes again, focus on the key words and what feelings are associated with these words. You might experience physical pain in some part of your body, which could be a sharp or stabbing pain, or tightness. Or perhaps you will experience emotional pain, such as sadness, or anger. As you explore the feeling, notice where this feeling settles in your body. Perhaps you sense a tightness in your chest, or in your throat, or you feel pain in your back. Experience the emotion fully. Allow it to flow through you without judgment, and write down what you observe. The feeling will most likely follow a trail to an event or a series of events in your life that are linked to that feeling. For example, let's take the feeling of being blamed for something, which was the strongest feeling for me. I feel tightness in my chest; my heart starts beating faster, and I feel nauseous. I write down what comes up, such as a fear of being punished because I've done some-thing wrong, I'm a bad girl, I'm worthless. Then I write down, the fear of not being loved, and, there it is, the fear that began it all. I was still holding on to the belief that if I do something wrong, the people around me will punish me and stop loving me.

When I wrote down those words, I was reminded of an event that happened when I was about five years old. We were visiting one of my older sisters who was away at college and, while we were in the waiting room, I was intrigued by a fancy ashtray on the coffee table. Yes, back then, there were ashtrays on coffee tables in public places. I picked it up, but I dropped it, and it fell on the floor and broke. The feeling I experienced at that moment obviously affected me greatly, and I judged myself all the way deep down into my subconscious. I felt like I had done something wrong, and I was afraid of being punished. I felt so worthless. I was scared. I had not thought about that moment in all these years, but it was at the beginning of this trail of events.

Looking back at my notes from previous exercises like this one (it's easier if you keep a notebook to write down each session), I noticed a commonality of being defensive and having to explain my words or actions. The people in all the events that I had explored to that point reflected back to me that I was still holding on to that scared, little girl who was afraid of being punished or blamed.

What you resist will continue to show up in your life through different people and situations until you release it. Each time you experience a situation that leaves you feeling bad, check in with your inner wisdom. This pattern, which began very early for me, continued throughout my life. I carried the belief of "I must have done something wrong, so I'm unlovable" into a series of events in my life.

Keep in mind that no one is to blame for making you feel bad, that this exercise is not about stating how wrong the other person was and wishing that he or she had behaved differently or that someone in your life now should change. It's about becoming the observer of the story—the witness, not the victim—and discovering what beliefs you are holding on to. After doing a few of these exercises, you may find a recurring theme like I did. The events will be different, and they might happen repeatedly with the same person or with different people, but the same phrases and beliefs will show up until you get the message and let it go.

Once you understand that it's all just a story and that you no longer need to blame the actors in your story because they just showed you the beliefs you were carrying around, you can end that story, say thank-you, and release the ego's hold on you. When you're able to say, "so what? It's not real; it's just a story that is no longer relevant in my life," the story is over. There is no need to keep that story alive. One final step that I find useful is to turn off the power I had assigned to that story, that belief, by visualizing pulling the plug or turning off a light switch.

You may also wish to try hypnotherapy. It is a helpful method to accomplish these results. Hypnosis is very natural. All hypnosis is self-hypnosis. We all experience it every day. Hypnosis is the same state of consciousness that you find yourself in just before falling asleep every night, when your brain waves go from beta to alpha to theta—when you are between wakefulness and sleep, feeling calm and deeply relaxed. In hypnosis, it is possible to reach all five levels of brain waves. You will go from beta, which is your normal, busy-thinking, waking consciousness, to alpha, where you are calm and relaxed, but alert, to theta, which is a deeper relaxation, closer to a meditative state, which is also where REM sleep happens. Delta is a very deep relaxation, deep dreamless sleep, and loss of body aware-ness. When you reach gamma, you have higher consciousness; feel-ings of peace, bliss, and joy; higher mental activity, perception, and problem solving. Hypnosis is just focused concentration.

In hypnotherapy, the therapist serves as a guide to help you relax, but your unconscious mind, your inner guardian, will safely take you as deeply as you need to go, to a significant moment where you can observe without reacting. That moment can sometimes be in a different lifetime or another parallel dimension, which I will discuss in a later chapter. In my practice, I found hypnosis to be a very useful tool to bypass the thinking mind, thereby eliminating judg-ment, and making it easier to access feelings. Since the conscious mind is reluctant to let go of control, it's important to put it at ease at the start of the session, to let it know that we are not trying to get rid of it, but just sending it on a picnic while we talk to the subconscious mind. The conscious mind is never not present, it's just quieter and more willing to release control for a while.

I have used self-hypnosis to work through many of my own life stories. It allows you to get out of your head and into your heart. As in the previous exercise, the hypnotherapist facilitates the conversation with your feelings, helping you to draw out what is already inside you, giving your feelings a voice, so you can see what they are linked to. They will often be linked to your childhood. That inner child has been stuck in a deep-seated belief and just needs to hear what was never said. Let your inner child speak and say what was never said to him (or her). From your heart, be the voice you needed when you were hurting, such as "I see you, I hear you, I understand you, and I love you. I am here you are not alone." Then acknowledge that there is no one to blame, that everyone was just playing their roles. That's when transformation happens—when you can experience this feeling fully and realize that it's not real; it's just a belief that is part of a story, and you can choose to let it go now. It has no relevance in your life today, and there's no benefit whatsoever in holding on to it. This acknowledgment will empower you to change the story.

Another helpful method to release emotions is called EFT, which stands for Emotional Freedom Techniques (sometimes called tapping). In essence, it is an emotional version of acupuncture, without the use of needles. The tapping stimulates certain meridian points on the body. I obtained a certificate of completion in 2001 from the founder of EFT, Gary Craig. He first introduced these techniques to the public in 1995. Since then, there have been many others who have created their own version of the techniques, so you will find hundreds of variations online.

Tapping is a practical modality I used with clients in my hypnotherapy practice, and I still use on myself today. Here is the EFT Tapping Basic Recipe as taught by Gary Craig.[19] In this method, there are nine tapping points. Tapping is normally done with two fingertips, but you can use three or four fingers if you wish. For some

19 The Gary Craig Official EFT, https://www.emofree.com/

of the tapping points, you can choose either the left or the right side; it's not necessary to tap on both sides.

1. The first step is to identify the issue that is bothering you, such as: sore shoulder, my boss put me down in front of my colleagues, fear of something, or a difficulty accomplishing a task. Focus on one issue at a time.

2. On a scale of zero to ten, zero being no pain and ten being the most intense, rate your pain or issue.

3. To set up before you begin tapping, come up with a phrase that describes your problem, such as "even though I have this (the problem you want to address), I deeply and completely accept myself."

4. Begin tapping on the side of the palm of your hand, what is called the Karate Chop point, while repeating your phrase three times.

5. Shorten your phrase to a reminder phrase that you will repeat as you move down your body to each tapping point. The reminder phrase might be "this sore shoulder" or "this fear of snakes." Repeat your reminder phrase three times as you tap on each point, starting at the top of your head, then moving down to the corner of your eyebrow, to the side of the eye (the bone next to the eye), on the bone under the eye, under the nose, on the chin point (between your bottom lip and the bottom of your chin), then at the beginning of the collarbone, and under the arm (about four inches under the armpit).

6. After the first round, assess the intensity on the scale of zero to ten to see if it has gone down.

7. Repeat the tapping sequence until you are either at zero, or have reached a plateau. If you have reached a plateau, it is

possible that there are other issues connected to the problem that you need to look at. This basic method is a wonderful and practical tool to use on the spot, in a variety of situations.

The next time you find yourself in an irritating or hurtful situation, instead of responding orally, do your best to remain silent, and listen to your thoughts. Be aware of your inner wisdom; it is trying to show you something about yourself that you are resisting. Before speaking, ask your inner self to let you know if or when it's wise to respond, and what is the best response. The ego wants to distract you by persuading you to look *out there* for the cause of your pain or discomfort. It wants you to blame someone else and it would have you believe that the other person should stop behaving that way and stop making you feel bad. If you find that your ego is interpreting and judging the person or situation, be the noncritical observer. Your inner wisdom wants you to look within to find the source of the irritation and to realize that no one is to blame for how you feel. Emotions are not bad; it's your addiction to them that's the problem.

Recognition of the Habit Is the Key

Once you recognize the belief and you drop it, it's gone. Awareness is the first step. Become aware of the self-limiting, fear-based beliefs, and say thank-you to that fear for showing up, because it's showing you what you're still holding onto. Once you realize that these beliefs are just part of the story, you can begin to transform your life. Sometimes, you may find that, just when you thought you had cleared a problem, your higher self will send you a pop quiz, so you can face an issue one more time. Time is not in a straight line; it is a spiral, so you may encounter a situation again, giving you an opportunity to discover its deeper truth.

Everything you need to be free will show up on the path right in front of you in the present. You don't necessarily have to go searching in your past to find the reasons. You can if you want to. I helped many people explore that option in my practice. If searching your past helps clear the story, go for it. But if you don't, no worries; your bus driver will let someone on the bus to play that role perfectly right here in the present. When you live in the moment, what you need to know will be there when you need to know it. In this moment, right now, where are the past and the future? Nowhere; a word that can be read as nowhere or now here!

There is only now. We don't need a story. The ego needs a story. It is the one attaching importance to an experience. What if the past is just a story created by the ego to justify that fear or guilt, that sadness or anger? No matter when something happened, our power to change is right now. Our intent to heal is right now, and all the information we need to change that vibration is here right now.

Whatever we are still holding on to will be shown to us in the here and now, and our reaction in that moment will determine if we continue to carry the baggage or if we drop it at the bus stop. As we become non-reactive, we detach from the story. We are transformed, and we realize that there is nothing that needs to be fixed.

In *Communion with God*, Neale Donald Walsh reminds us to use this formula when facing any life experience:

1. Nothing in my world is real.

2. The meaning of everything is the meaning I give it.

3. I am who I say I am, and my experience is what I say it is.

Reality is always a question mark. Every thought we have, and everything we do has only the meaning we give it, based on our beliefs and judgments. To quote American mythologist, Joseph Campbell, "[I]ife is without meaning. You bring the meaning to it. The meaning of life is whatever you ascribe it to be. Being alive is the meaning"[20]

---

20 https://www.brainyquote.com/quotes/joseph_campbell_133214

As proven by quantum mechanics, at the quantum level, reality does not exist if we are not looking at it. Reality doesn't exist until it is being observed, or measured. We don't see reality as it is; we create a story according to our perception of it. Once we make that story real in our mind, it becomes our reality. We see what we need to see when we need to see it. It is wise to take our perceptions seriously, but not to take them literally. We can compare our physical reality to the interface of a computer desktop. The desktop represents space, and the icons represent physical objects. It's important to take the objects or icons seriously, but not literally. We constructed them to accomplish a task. The true reality of the desktop is the interface where the complexity of our world is hidden.

Since we are all members of the same species and work with the same symbols that we have come to agree upon, we accept what we see as real. If we all agree that we see a train, it must be true, and it must be real. If we all agree that we see a cliff in front of us, we won't jump off and get hurt. These symbols are designed to keep us safe and alive within this reality, this story. Space and time exist for that purpose.

Our egos want to keep us in the illusion, but we can step out of the illusion at any time and become an observer. You are an actor, but you are also the audience member, the impartial observer. Become aware of the character you are playing in the play of life, and, at the same time, monitor your performance. See yourself through the eyes of the ultimate observer. You are in this world, but not of this world.

Your thoughts become important to you only because you allow them into your mind and give them attention. You attract thoughts to yourself that originate mostly in other minds. There is something in you that attracts these thoughts, and they eventually become your words and your beliefs, which eventually become manifestations in your life. Your thoughts bind you; your fears limit you; and your beliefs control you. So, stand guard at the door of your mind, and allow only thoughts or feelings that you want to manifest in your life. Pay attention to what you've been telling yourself and others, for it will become your reality.

Energy flows where attention goes. According to quantum physics, everything is a wave of unlimited possibilities of what can happen, and when observed, particles come together to create a reality. What you put your attention on, what you observe, collapses the wave to manifest your reality. Thoughts are the electrical charge in the quantum field, and feelings are the magnetic charge. The quantum field responds to who we are, not to what we want. What food is to the body, feelings are to the soul.

CHAPTER 7

STOP TAKING YOURSELF SO SERIOUSLY, NO ONE ELSE DOES

It's not necessary to know why something happened the way it did. Asking why will only keep you inside the box, slow you down, and prevent you from moving on. The only reason for anything is the one you give it, so you can decide what the reason means. However you interpret the reason, it is just a made-up story. What does it matter? How important is it to know the reason right now? As the Buddhist Parable of the Poisoned Arrow goes, "[s]uppose a man is struck by a poisoned arrow and the doctor wishes to take out the arrow immediately. Suppose the man does not want the arrow removed until he knows who shot it, his age, his parents, and why he shot it...until he knows his home village, town or city...until he knows whether the bow was a long bow or a crossbow...until he knows whether the feathers of the shaft were those or a vulture, a hawk, a peacock, or another bird..."[21] What does it matter? How important is it to know the answers to these questions right then and there? The man could die while searching and waiting for answers. If I had wanted such answers before the surgeon inserted chest tubes due to my

21 https://en.wikipedia.org/wiki/Parable_of_the_Poisoned_Arrow

collapsed lungs following the motorcycle accident, I would have died. If there are circumstances in your life that are creating stress and you know that what is happening is not healthy for you, how much more information do you need before you choose to do something?

Ask yourself how important whatever you are feeling depressed, guilty, or angry about right now will be in five years, a hundred years, or a thousand years? Ask yourself, if this was your last day on this earth, would it be worth wasting your time being angry?

Thanks to the ego, human beings have a habit of taking themselves very seriously. We put too much importance on what others might think because that's what our ego has been telling us all along. Well, other people's opinion of you is none of your business. As Dr. Abraham Maslow states, "[b]e independent of the good opinion of other people."[22] It's just their opinion; it's not real. Don't let someone else define who you are. It's okay to be you and to experience pleasure. You are here to enjoy life. Whatever you do, enjoy it fully, even if you spend time doing nothing. Enjoy doing so without feeling guilty.

The ride to discovering who you are is meant to be exciting and joyful. As far back as I can remember, I have always sought answers. In my childhood, my personal search included religion, but I didn't find any answers there. It seemed incomplete, so, as a teenager, I became much more interested in spirituality than religion. I found meaning that resonated with me, and I saw significant differences between spirituality and religion. Spirituality is the personal search to find the greater meaning in life and one's existence in this world. It's your personal relationship with creation. It is the bridge between your mind, body, and spirit. Religion is basically an intermediary, and I always prefer to go directly to the source, not hearsay or someone's interpretation, to get my answers. Transformation happens through direct experience, not by simply believing in a teacher or leader. Your real and only teacher is your divine self. Deepak

22 https://www.azquotes.com/quote/481913

Chopra, an alternative-medicine advocate, asserts that "[r]eligion is belief in someone else's experience. Spirituality is having your own experience."[23] That makes the ride so much more exciting!

Religion builds walls. Its rules and constrictions have turned spirituality into dogma. It would have us believe that we are separate from the infinite intelligence that created us, that we need a go-between to connect with our creator, and that the only way back is through the church. It even has us competing for God among the different religions. Most humans have an innate desire to connect with a higher power. And guess what? You are already connected and always have been. The illusion is that we are separate from this divine source. I understood this at a very young age, and that is why I quickly lost interest in religion. I was raised in the Catholic faith, and as an adult, I explored the teachings of other traditions. Some of them resonated with me, but I wanted to connect in my own way because I knew that this higher power was already inside me. We are like birds flying high, trying to reach the sky, while all the time being in the sky.

You have a direct line of communication because you are an expression of the life force. This life force is within you. So, you don't need to be in a special building to feel the connection. No matter where you are, it is a sacred space. You may no longer feel the need to go to church or to religious gatherings of any kind to find God. When you go within, you find the life force there, it is never not present.

Most people consider their religion or their spirituality meaningful, but does it really have to be so serious? Who made these rules? God is not sitting on a throne somewhere in the clouds, looking down, and shaking his finger at us. Many people believe that to be spiritual and good we have to make sacrifices, and deny ourselves the pleasures of our physical bodies and the physical world. Being good has nothing to do with obeying laws. God does not have an

23 https://www.quotenova.net/authors/deepak-chopra/q6742e

agenda; he does not need anything from us nor does he grant or deny wishes. God is not Santa Claus, bringing you presents if you've been good. Some people believe that by joining and supporting a religious or spiritual organization, they will please God and they will then receive special favors from him. There is nothing we have to do—no sacrifices, no rituals, no rules to obey—to please God. God is already pleased with you. God is your own true self. Rather than being controlled by mortal laws, trust in your inner wisdom to help you decide what is loving and ethical. Freedom doesn't have any rules. Rules hold you back. Just because certain rituals have been a certain way in your lifetime and in your family, do not feel obligated to continue practicing them. Do what resonates with you now. If something limits you, let it go. It's time to let go of the outdated interpretation of the Adam and Eve story in the Garden of Eden. It's time to discover the Tree of Life and to remember who you really are.

Just because something is meaningful, it doesn't mean it can't be fun or funny. Several years ago, I was in a spiritual group in Fort Myers, Florida, and one day we were on the subject of our physical bodies, our vehicle for this earth-life experience. I mentioned during our discussion that, "I see my body as my temple and treat it as such. I exercise and I eat well." Someone in the group added, "then I would have to say that my body is more like a circus tent." We all had a good laugh. Yes, I still treat my body as my temple, but I also take it to the circus once in a while. I think that anything worth taking seriously is worth making fun of.

I spent almost fifty years of my life taking myself and my spirituality quite seriously. When my life was turned upside down, I decided it was time to change the way I looked at things. In the words of Max Planck and Dr. Wayne Dyer, "[w]hen you change the way you look at things, the things you look at change."[24] When my

24 https://www.wisefamousquotes.com/max-planck-quotes/
when-you-change-the-way-you-look-at-749906/
https://www.drwaynedyer.com/blog/success-secrets/

life turned upside down I had the option of looking at the situation as a total disaster, giving up, and drowning in despair, or getting back up, and starting moving. I decided that having a great sense of humor would be a great asset. I had to be able to see the humor in all this.

It's Just a Ride

In his routine "It's Just a Ride,"[25] American stand-up comedian Bill Hicks compared life to an amusement park ride. You go up and down and around, sometimes you're upside down, sometimes you're up on top with your arms in the air, enjoying the view from a different perspective. No one is better or worse, or more advanced than someone who's in front, or behind, or upside down. We're all at a different point of the ride.

When I found myself with no job, no money, no husband, and no place to call home, that was my moment at the top of the roller-coaster hill, that moment when I had stopped climbing the first part of what seemed like a very long, strenuous hill, and had arrived at that scary 'what do I do now' moment. Well, it was time to let go of the fear and the resistance I had carried to that point. There was no time to think and analyze like I had always done. It was time to put my arms up, go with it, and just trust in the sacred energy that was guiding me—be in the moment, buckle up, and enjoy the ride.

I noticed that even though I was without all my material stuff, the stuff I thought I needed, I was still here; I still existed. I have heard people say that they are afraid they will lose everything if they decide to leave a situation or partner. I've been there. I lost it all, and I'm okay. The fact that I'm still here is evidence that I was provided with what I needed to get to my next step. You can always get more stuff; the stores are full of it. If you find yourself in a dark place in your

---

25 https://youtu.be/KgzQuElpR1w

life, remind yourself that darkness is just a shadow that indicates the direction of the light.

Don't let fear take your freedom away, shut you down, or punish you. Follow your inner excitement. There is no need to make things happen. Leave the planning to your higher mind. Follow what brings you joy. When you feel motivated to act on your passion, do it. You don't have to know all the details, or the when, and the how. You don't have to understand it all at the conscious level, just be open and willing. Take the first step, stay in the excitement, and you will be linked to the next step. I like what Martin Luther King Jr. said about faith, "[T]ake the first step in faith. You don't have to see the whole staircase, just take the first step."[26] So, take the first step, stay in the excitement, and you will be linked to the next step. Excitement means you're on the right path for you, that you're being who you really are. Faith is believing in something when common sense tells you not to. Trust that you always make the right choice. Do not analyze; do not try to figure out how an event is going to happen. It's not your responsibility to control the outcome. Lack of faith comes down to a belief that you are not worthy of having the life that you desire, which results in fear. Keep your mind free from doubts and worries, and leave the details to your divine self. Trust that you will be provided with what you need to get to the next step. I had no idea what I was going to do following the accident in 2003 or after losing everything in 2010, but as I moved forward one step at a time, I trusted my higher self and was provided with what I needed. I continue to remind myself every day to trust that it's all going to work out, and it always has, and it always does. One of my favorite sayings is "this too shall pass." Be willing to press the reset button, and be open to new opportunities.

When we let go of resistance and go with the flow of passion and excitement, we are in alignment with our true selves, and life becomes effortless. Instead of thinking that you can't do something,

26 https://www.azquotes.com/author/8044-Martin_Luther_King_Jr

change that thought to, "what if this time I can?" Enter into a partnership with your higher mind, row your boat gently down the stream, not up the stream, and you will be filled with soul-satisfying experiences. Oh, and remember to row your boat gently down your stream, not someone else's. Something I learned along the way.

Helping others has always been and still is a natural aspect of my being, but I no longer think that there's something wrong with people that needs to be fixed. I prefer to allow others to be, and do, and go as they wish, without interfering. That takes priority over being right or dominating others. Everyone is doing and being exactly who and what they are supposed to do and be in every moment. We are not broken. We are perfect as we are. If I have uplifting or insightful information to share with someone and it brings me joy to do so, I share it. It could be the message they were ready to hear. I trust that if I can be the messenger in someone's life, that person will cross my path at the perfect moment, and sometimes they will have a message for me. Some people cross our path to reflect something back to us about ourselves, and sometimes they show up to set something in motion that will support us in whatever we are doing.

Let's Talk about Compassion

Is compassion just another layer of the ego? Well, that depends on the intention and motivation behind your actions.

While focusing your attention on trying to relieve the suffering of others might seem like the caring thing to do, it's quite arrogant of the ego to think that it knows what's best for that person. How do you know what that person should be experiencing? Others have their own circus, their own monkeys. Their experiences have been created specifically for them, and they will deal with their own lessons when they are ready. You can show support for someone, but you do not have to carry the weight for them. At times, a situation will require action on your part, but in some cases, it will be wise to remain quiet. Trust that a higher mind knows the bigger picture and knows what that person needs in his or her story. You can never change anyone, and it's not your responsibility to change them.

In my second marriage, I thought it was my duty to change my partner, and I took it upon myself to point out what he needed to change and what he should do. My intentions were good. I was convinced that I knew what was best for him. Looking back now, I know that I had no business messing with his circus and his monkeys.

People will point out a sad situation and comment on how bad sad, or sorry they feel for the people involved. No matter how sad or sorry you feel for them, know that no amount of sadness on your part will alleviate the sadness in someone's else life experience. No amount of feeling bad for someone will make them feel better. No amount of worry about someone will make that person safe. When you can observe someone's suffering without judging it as wrong, needing to change or without feeling bad for them, you can take action because you're happy to do it. I'm often reminded of that when I see someone begging for money on the street, and I realize that I don't have to give them money, but I don't have to judge them. You can jump in and help someone out of a situation or you can empower them by giving them the tools to pull themselves up. Do something because you choose to, not because you think you have to. Notice your intention next time you're feeling compassionate. Everything you do, you are doing for yourself.

As long as you are busy trying to fix everyone's problems, you are not looking at yourself. It is your responsibility to live your own reality, to process your own judgments, beliefs, opinions, and fears. You are here to witness your own life and to become aware of your reactions. The best thing you can do is be a model for others. When you raise your vibration, everyone benefits. The same thing applies to the idea of saving the world; it's just another game of the ego to maintain its existence.

Most of us have sent our good wishes and prayers to our loved ones or to the people involved in a situation in the world. Note that even though we appear separate from one another, communication is instantaneous. It's not necessary to send anything anywhere. Your prayers don't leave from you and are not carried to another location. The moment you focus on your wishes and prayers for someone, they are instantly received. Your consciousness and the other person's consciousness are connected. There is only now. Everything is now.

Intuition

Intuition means to be taught from within. It is your inner navigation system. It is a voice inside you that has always been there. It is not based on reasoning; it is a knowing that comes all at once. We are all born with it, but it must be developed, just like a muscle, to make it stronger.

Intuition can be experienced through different senses. Some people will get a clear vision of a situation that could be happening down the street or even several miles away, beyond what their physical eyes could see. They will get an internal vision in what is referred to as the mind's eye. This is called clairvoyance or clear seeing.

Others are more auditory and will get intuitive messages as an inner voice, heard directly in the brain or that seems to come from behind the person in front of them. This voice will often have an authoritarian tone. This is known as clairaudience or clear hearing. This is not the same as hearing voices in your head, which could come from your conscious mind or from someone else's mind. Clear hearing is quite different, and you know it when it happens. I had a profound clairaudience experience with a client in my office one day. We were sitting facing each other, having a discussion after a hypnotherapy session, when I sensed a powerful presence standing behind him. There seemed to be a group of five beings in spirit form. The one in the middle spoke to me in a kind, but very authoritarian, tone. I could hear his voice clearly, although not with my physical ears. He had messages for me and my client. My client could not hear this voice, but the messages I relayed made complete sense to him. As this spiritual being spoke, the walls, the ceiling, and the floor of my office seemed to disappear, and it felt as though my client and I were suspended somewhere in the universe. We had no sense of space or time. When the conversation ended, we were back in my office, and two hours had gone by.

The most frequent way individuals experience intuition is through hunches or gut feelings. This is known as clairsentience, clear sensing, or feeling. When you get a sense of knowing that comes from within, when you just know without a doubt that you are supposed to act a certain way, no matter what others are telling you, you should follow that knowing. Some people are also very sensitive to another person's energy or vibration and know whether to engage with that person or situation or to walk away.

Other modes of intuition include clairolfaction, the ability to smell the essence of a substance, and clairgustance, the ability to perceive the essence of a substance through taste. Perhaps there was a time when you made the decision to not do something because, when you thought about it, "it just left a bad taste in your mouth."

I remember one day, as I was sitting quietly at home reading, when, all of a sudden, I felt the presence of my aunt Evelyne, who had passed away several years before. She was my father's sister. For some reason, I had been thinking about her. Within seconds of undeniably feeling her presence in the room and before I could say anything, my husband said, "Do you smell that?" I turned to him and replied, "I was about to ask you the same thing." There was a definite smell of a delightful perfume in the house. I shared with him that I could feel my aunt's presence, like she had just come for a visit and had walked across our living room, letting me know that all was well. Her presence lasted for a few minutes, then she was gone and so was the lovely scent. There was no one else in the house, and there were no candles burning.

Intuition can also be experienced as telepathy, being able to communicate through thought transference. How many times have you thought of someone you haven't heard from in a while, and they call you shortly after? Start paying attention to your intuitive messages, and observe how often you are correct. Just like any other skill, the more you practice, the easier it becomes.

Some people are able to intuitively obtain information from holding an object that belongs to someone. This is known as psychometry. It is possible to get feelings, sensations, thoughts, or visions from holding the object.

Learning to recognize and interpret your intuitive messages is very useful whenever you want to know what's right for you. These messages will be your inspired truth, not someone else's. No one knows what's best for someone else. Intuition is listening to your soul. Words and thoughts will come from others, and they will beg to enter your mind, so it's wise to learn how to recognize them as such. In the words of Socrates, "[e]veryone tells you what to do and what's good for you. They don't want you to find your own answers. They want you to believe theirs."[27] Instead of letting other people's words and thoughts gain entry into your mind, ask your own infinite intelligence for help with any situation you are facing. No matter how impossible a situation might seem, your infinite intelligence knows the way out. For example, you can ask, "what is important for me to know about this situation, or what is the best way to approach this situation, or what would my infinite self do?" You will be given the answer. You may sense it, see it, or hear it, but however you receive the answer, you will be pointed in the right direction. Listen to your intuition, and be open to receive the messages you need.

---

27 https://medium.com/@wanha/13-quotes-from-gandhi-to-socrates-to-challenge-your-life-assumptions-d102145d27a6

The day I chose to move in with, and later marry, my first husband, my mother was totally against it. I had to defend my decision and justify what was in my heart. There was a strong feeling within me that I could not explain why this had to be. I just knew it was the right thing for me at that moment. There was no talking me out of it. It wasn't something I wanted to do just to make my mother sad or angry. I have always had a strong intuition, and it has always guided me exactly where I am supposed to be. In the twenty-six years we were married, he played his role perfectly to reflect back to me what I needed to see. That was not a decision anyone else could have made for me because how does anyone know what's best for someone else?

From personal experience, I know that every time I have ignored my intuition, situations didn't turn out so well, such as when I had the near fatal motorcycle accident. I remember another time when my ex and I had gone to Atlanta, Georgia, for a business meeting. When we arrived at the location, I had a very uneasy feeling about where we had parked the car alongside the building. I thought we should have parked it on the street right in front of the store, within view of where we were sitting. We didn't want to be late for our meeting, so I let it go, and we went about our business. After our meeting, we walked outside and found our car windows smashed to pieces, and items had been stolen from the back seat.

This guidance also applies when I meet people for the first time, whether it's in a business or a personal situation. I have noticed that my first five-second impression of someone always turns out to be accurate. The ego will often jump in immediately to distract me with what it thinks I should see or hear because it doesn't trust information coming from a source that it doesn't understand. It will do everything it can to persuade me to ignore that first impression. This game will work for a while, and everything will seem fine. The more hopeful I become by listening to the ego, the further away that first impression gets pushed, but it's still there, waiting patiently, and eventually, it makes its way back to the front of the line. Each time

I ignore my intuition, I find out later that it was accurate and that an unpleasant situation could have been avoided. Never argue with your intuition.

My mentor, Barbara, told me that, from the time she was a child, she knew that she had the gift of clairvoyance. However, she had never used it. One day, she had a vision of her six-year-old son crossing the road and getting hit by a car. As was her custom, she ignored that vision and went on with her daily life. A few months later, her vision became a reality, and her son was hit by a car and killed. From that moment on, she made a commitment to never ignore her intuition again, and she has made it her life mission to use her gift to help as many people as she could.

Have you ever been to a place for the first time and felt like you had been there before, or have you met someone for the first time and felt an instant, unexplainable, recognition, attraction, or animosity? I remember the first time I went to visit Chichen Itza in Mexico. The tour bus driver dropped the group off at a site's back entrance, where we followed a trail lined with tall trees that blocked the view of the grounds. When we reached the end of the trail, I looked up; we were right there behind the pyramid. It was as if it appeared out of nowhere from another time, another realm. I had such a strong emotional reaction. I could not stop the tears from flowing down my face, and I felt such an exhilarating feeling in my heart. I knew I had been there before. The feeling just intensified the entire time we were there. I've never had such a profound experience at any other place I've ever visited.

As I mentioned previously, when I met my first husband, I just knew we were supposed to be together, but I didn't know why. What was interesting was that when we were first introduced, I was repulsed. I had strong hatred toward him, and again, I had no idea why. It was very strange, but before long, there was an undeniable pull between us, and we started spending more time together. Throughout the years, a small part of me continued to feel that animosity. Only when

I decided to explore that feeling through hypnotherapy did I learn why. I discovered a lifetime, when we had also been husband and wife, during which he had come home drunk and killed me. We had two children, and I was pregnant at the time. As I relived that scene and watched myself leave my body, from a higher perspective, I got a better understanding of the situation. I was able to understand and forgive him, but my last words, as I left that life behind, were, "I will never have children with that man again." That experience explains why, from the beginning of our relationship in this current life, I had made it very clear to him that I never wanted to have children. I felt strongly about that, even though I wasn't exactly sure why at the time.

There was an instant, unexplainable recognition when I first met my second husband. As I explained earlier, we felt such a strong attraction and connection like we had known each other for a long time. Through hypnosis, we discovered that we had lived other lifetimes together. In one of them, he had had to leave with other soldiers, and I never saw him again. No wonder we were so happy to reconnect when we first saw each other in this current life. It was like, "where did you go? Where have you been all this time?" It also explains why I was always afraid of losing him when we were together. I had a feeling that he would disappear again someday, and I would never see him again.

Karma Is Also a Belief System

Karma is a Sanskrit word that means action, work, or deed. With origins in ancient India, karma is a key concept in Hinduism, Buddhism, Jainism, Sikhism, and Taoism. It also refers to the spiritual principle of cause and effect where the intent and action of an individual (cause) influence the future of that individual (effect). Good intent and good deed contribute to good karma and future happiness, while bad intent and bad deed contribute to bad karma and future suffering.[28]

In Roman Catholic theology, the place of purification of bad deeds is called purgatory and is an intermediate state after physical death in which some of those ultimately destined for heaven must first undergo purification, before entering heaven. The word purgatory has also come to refer to a wide range of historical and modern conceptions of postmortem suffering short of everlasting damnation and is used, in a nonspecific sense, to mean any place or condition of suffering or torment.[29]

What if karma and purgatory are just another couple of belief systems that have been created for our experience in this consciousness? They would be just like space and time, which are unreal functions also created for this consciousness. You've heard of the saying, *seeing is believing* or you might say that *believing is seeing*, so if you believe in the law of cause and effect, that's what you will see in action all around you.

Don't feel threatened by the everlasting punishments of the church. Karma is not about punishment or vengeance. There is no debt to be paid, no punishment or cleansing. That's what your ego wants you to believe so that you will keep punishing yourself, and others. The ego, wrapped up in its self-importance, is very much invested in this cause-and-effect interpretation of life. It seeks revenge and punishment. Punishment and consequences are not the same thing. You make a choice, which will be followed by a consequence. The consequence can be the result of a choice that was made last week, last year, or even in a different lifetime, and you may have no conscious memory of making that choice. Since everything is stored at the unconscious level and time does not exist at that level, it makes no difference when a choice was made. Choice and consequence exist at the unconscious level all at once.

---

28 https://simple.wikipedia.org/wiki/Karma
29 https://en.wikipedia.org/wiki/Purgatory

All experiences are blessings. They are not tests or karmic debts of previous acts. Karma is just a mechanism to let you know when you are out of alignment with the real you. What we experience as karma is simply our higher self, showing us a situation so we can experience both sides of it, understand how it feels, and make a choice to change. Karma can simply be used as an opportunity for enlightenment, to bring yourself back into balance—moving from fear toward love, finding the perfect balance. That's all. Karma brings your thoughts and actions to your attention, to inspire you to bring yourself back in alignment with the real you. To remember who you really are, you must first remember that this life experience is all make-believe, that the illusion you are in is not real. The illusion was intended for the purpose of creating context within which to experience who you really are. Use it that way. It is but a game being played by consciousness, in consciousness, and for consciousness. Beyond this level of consciousness, there is only understanding, love, and embrace.

CHAPTER 8

FROM SELF-IMPROVEMENT
TO SELF-ACCEPTANCE

I spent the first half of this human movie focused on self-improvement. I'm spending the second half on self-acceptance. Our egos would have us believe that self-improvement will eventually bring us happiness, but no matter how much self-improvement we do, it will not make up for the lack of self-acceptance. Self-acceptance is letting go of the ego and accepting your happiness, your love, and your peace.

Respect and love yourself, your body. Do what makes you feel good. Love and accept yourself just the way you are. Your body, your emotions, they're all perfect, and so is everyone else's. Accept that we're all different. Give yourself and others permission to just be, and you will no longer have the need to judge, blame, and criticize yourself or others. You will find that you no longer have the need to be right and the need to make anyone else wrong. You will replace the tendency to dominate with one of allowing others to choose what's best for them. Everyone has a strong sense of what they want and what their limits are. That applies to all people in your life, including your children. In the words of the poet Kahlil Gibran:

Your children are not your children.
They are the sons and daughters of Life's longing
for itself.
They come through you but not from you...[30]

When you become aware that you are being judgmental of
yourself or others and you're about to impose a rule, consider saying
nothing. Instead, switch to observing your feelings and actions. Be at
peace with what you observe. Instead of reacting in a defensive way
when you notice an irritating person or situation, just be with the
feeling you experience in that moment, and accept whatever comes
without labeling or defending it. Simply pay attention to the feeling
moving through your body without judging it. Become the observer
of the character you are playing. Monitor your performance, and ask
yourself, "what's the most loving thing I can do or say here?"

What if you stopped interfering and allowed life to unfold as it
should? What if you trusted that the same intelligence that is directing the universe is also guiding and directing you and everyone else
without your having to interfere? Instead of going through the rule
book to decide what's right, try closing it, and observe your life experiences fall perfectly into place. As a result, you will become more
loving, kinder, more respectful, more powerful, more mindful, and
that's what will be reflected back to you. What do you want to see in
the mirror?

How many conflicts in the world are the result of government
trying to control and conquer and meddle in everyone's lives? What
if natural resources, oceans, and animals were respected and allowed
to unfold as nature intended?

30 https://poets.org/poem/children-1

What about All the Negative Stuff Happening in the World?

You don't get peace by hating war; you get peace by loving peace. The more we resist something, the more of it will keep showing up in our lives. When we hate something, we are judging it and creating resistance. We cannot solve a problem with the same energy that created it. The more we participate in the fight against something, the more we continue to create resistance. In the words of Mother Teresa, "I was once asked why I didn't participate in anti-war demonstrations. I said that I will never do that, but as soon as you have a pro-peace rally, I'll be there."[31]

Everything is neutral; we give meaning to specific things with our beliefs and judgments. The story you tell yourself becomes your reality. What you believe makes it true, and you act accordingly. What we consider evil is simply based on the ego's judgment. To see something as it really is, we must let go of our judgments. Whether we think what we see is good or bad doesn't matter at all. All that matters is seeing it as it is. We don't change the world we are in; the world is a reflection of the changes we have made within ourselves. What we observe as pain and suffering is an opportunity for us to do something about us, to leave judgment behind. In the words of Shakespeare, "[n]othing is good or bad, but thinking makes it so."[32]

What if we don't need to be fixed or saved? What if the earth doesn't need to be saved either? What if everything is exactly the way it's supposed to be? The physical world is part of the illusion. The illusion seems real because our belief that it is supports the illusion. The moment we believe it is real, the illusion turns into fear.

When I was a teenager, one of my sisters gave me an album entitled *Desiderata*. Desiderata (Latin: desired things) is a 1927 prose

---

31 https://www.azquotes.com/author/14530-Mother_Teresa/tag/war
32 http://www.finestquotes.com/quote-id-4136.htm

poem by American writer Max Ehrmann. I am reminded of the last verse of that poem.

> And whether or not it is clear to you, no doubt the universe is unfolding as it should. Therefore, be at peace with God, whatever you conceive Him to be. And whatever your labors and aspirations, in the noisy confusion of life, keep peace in your soul. With all its sham, drudgery and broken dreams, it is still a beautiful world. Be cheerful. Strive to be happy.[33]

Just as the lotus flower lives within the sludge of a dirty swamp without being tainted by it, you can grow and be beautiful without being affected by the dirt around you.

Your infinite self allows your soul to express itself through your human personality, without limitation. Your soul creates circumstances or challenges, but it does not create your pain and suffering, your resistance to your life experiences does. When you experience pain, your judgment of that experience causes suffering. The purpose of these experiences is to help raise your awareness of the meaning behind them and to release judgment.

Keep peace in your soul by letting go of resistance. When you go with the flow instead of resisting, life becomes effortless. Focus on expressing your true identity. Whatever shows up for you, do it the best you know how.

In a World of Duality

We live in a world of duality. The belief system we have carried with us since the story of Adam and Eve promotes duality and judgment. We went from having eternal life to experiencing death, from having abundance to not having enough, to living the illusion that there is a beginning and an end. This story promotes duality, meaning

---

33 https://www.desiderata.com/desiderata.html

two-ism or seeing the whole as somehow divided. Similarly, the word divided has two parts: di like duo means two, and vided means seen; together, they mean seeing two.

With yin and yang, everything occurs in pairs of opposites, but the opposites always function in unity. We learn through contrast. For us to know beauty, we must also know the concept of ugliness. To know if someone is tall, he or she must be compared to a short person, and vice versa. All these beliefs depend on opposites. Opposites give meaning to each other. Male is the opposite of female; happiness is the opposite of suffering, and life is the opposite of death. We must experience one to know the other. Both are essential and inseparable. Darkness and light, left and right, front and back, up and down, hot and cold, water and ice, heaven and hell, cannot be separated. They are the same thing at different degrees of vibration. At what exact point does light become darkness and vice versa? What we refer to as the condition of something makes it appear different to us. That condition is true at the moment we observe it, but when conditions change, truth changes. Think about how the astronauts' definition of up and down disappears when conditions change in outer space.

When we accept both opposites, without criticism, we realize that they are perfect oneness, coexisting in this illusion of duality. Accept both sides, without judgment, and let the illusion be.

Accept that we are both a human personality, and a perfect divine being coexisting in this illusion of duality. We have free will to make choices, and choices are made for us at the same time. We are free to choose, but we are not free from the consequence of our choice. We want to get what we want, and at the same time, we must surrender. This is the paradox we live in, and it is perhaps the reason for the smile on Buddha's face. We live in the universe, and the universe lives within us. This world of duality is a mystery that the human intellect has a hard time believing and accepting.

It is said that this mystery of division is a result of the spiritual war between Archangels Michael and Lucifer, the forces of light and darkness. Archangel Michael, whose name means *Who is like God*, reminds us how to listen to our inner wisdom. Lucifer means *Bearer of Light*, or *The Shining One*. He was the highest archangel, who had a desire to create, but in a different way than God's way, by introducing polarity consciousness into our physical reality. This gave man the ability to use his left brain to manipulate reality using logic as opposed to listening to his inner wisdom. Unfortunately, humans have become addicted to left-brain technology and have forgotten how to use their inner wisdom. Only when we combine our left brain, which is something outside of ourselves, and our intuitive right brain, which comes from within, can we recover our power and be in alignment in this world of duality.

The Truth Has Always Been Inside You

> *Remember, the entrance door to the sanctuary is inside you.*[34] — Rumi

Manifestation is not about attracting something to yourself from somewhere out there. It's about vibrating to the same frequency of what's already inside you. The truth has always been there, but it remains invisible to you until your frequency matches with it. It's not a secret.

> According to an old Hindu legend...
> There was once a time when all human beings were gods, but they so abused their divinity that Brahma, the chief god, decided to take it away from them and hide it where it could never be found.
> Where to hide their divinity was the question. So, Brahma called a council of the gods to help him decide. "Let's bury it deep in the earth," said the

---

34 https://www.azquotes.com/quote/752153

gods. But Brahma answered, "No, that will not do because humans will dig into the earth and find it." Then the gods said, "Let's sink it in the deepest ocean." But Brahma said, "No, not there, for they will learn to dive into the ocean and will find it." Then the gods said, "Let's take it to the top of the highest mountain and hide it there." But once again Brahma replied, "No, that will not do either, because they will eventually climb every mountain and once again take up their divinity." Then the gods gave up and said, "We do not know where to hide it, because it seems that there is no place on earth or in the sea that human beings will not eventually reach."

Brahma thought for a long time and then said, "Here is what we will do. We will hide their divinity deep in the center of their own being, for humans will never think to look for it there." All the gods agreed that this was the perfect hiding place, and the deed was done. And since that time humans have been going up and down the earth, digging, diving, climbing, and exploring—searching for something already within themselves[35]

The truth you seek is within you. Throughout our earth stories that have become religious doctrine, many have died for speaking this truth; some were even crucified. Those who judge do so because they are afraid, afraid of losing control. They still believe the stories, based on fear, that have been so ingrained, that sins must have consequences and must be punished in the name of their god and religion.

Back in 1945, in a cave near Nag Hammadi in the upper Egyptian desert, fifty-two papyrus texts of gospels were found by an

---

35 http://www.naute.com/stories/hideout.phtml

Arab peasant. They are a collection of texts, known as the Gnostic Gospels, that were written between the second and fourth centuries after Jesus' death. Gnostic is a Greek word meaning knowledge. The writings describe events from a different point of view than what is found in the four gospels in the New Testament. These gospels were considered heresy and, therefore, were abolished by the orthodox church. By the fourth century, possession of such writings became a criminal offense, and copies of such books were burned. Fortunately, not all of them were destroyed. Some were hidden in the cave only to be found 1,600 years later.

The orthodox church says that humans are separate from the creator, and that Jesus, the Son of God, who is not like humans, came to save us from our sins. In contrast, the Gnostic Gospels say that Jesus and humans come from the same source, and that the presence of the divine is within us, that Jesus came as a spiritual guide to enlighten us, so we could see through the illusion and become equals. In the texts, the human being is referred to as a spiritual being walking a human pathway.

There are no secrets that God doesn't want you to know. You already know who you really are, and you are here to remember. Jesus' message was to reawaken people to the Garden of Eden consciousness. If you look at the metaphysical interpretation of the stories of the Bible, you will find the answers.

Holy scriptures have been written to show humans how to release their souls from bondage. Every civilization has written about its spiritual mysteries, designed to help us reawaken our true spiritual essence. In the Western world, the search to remember our true spiritual essence, is referred to as the quest for the Holy Grail. American philosopher, Ernest Holmes stated that "[t]he great spiritual geniuses, whether it was Moses, Buddha, Plato, Socrates, Jesus, or Emerson...have taught man to look within himself to find God."[36]

36 https://www.azquotes.com/quote/813444

Your Life's Purpose Is to Master Yourself

One can have no smaller or greater mastery than mastery of oneself.[37] — Leonardo da Vinci

It was right there in front of me or, should I say, inside me all along. I went to the bottom of the ocean, and I climbed to the top of the mountain. I searched and searched to discover my life's purpose, believing that it had to come from something outside of me, that it had to be something grand, to be the most famous this or that. We hear so much about finding our life's purpose that we tend to believe that unless we are doing something grand, we have not found our purpose, and therefore we must not be good enough. That is a myth. Perhaps, sharing your gifts or just being a positive influence in the lives of others around you is your life's purpose. I used to believe that unless I was actively working in a metaphysical field I would not be evolving spiritually. That's also a myth. So is thinking that the only way to grow spiritually is through struggling. Sure, there are always opportunities to grow in difficult times, but there are other ways. Another misconception is thinking that once you find your spiritual purpose, everything else in your life will be perfect.

I realized that my only purpose is to master myself; it is not to fix others, but to be my greatest version of myself in each moment and to fulfill my passion for writing. Even though I have not been working in the metaphysical field for many years and had put my studies on hold, I now recognize that I was still growing and evolving. It's perfectly fine to take a rest from exploration occasionally, and when you pick it back up, you may be pleasantly surprised that you are further along the path than you thought. All my life experiences until now were designed to help me fulfill my calling, each provided an understanding that I can now share and perhaps help someone on their journey.

---

37 https://www.goalcast.com/2018/04/03/leonardo-da-vinci-quotes/

My search had, deep down, always been about the search for happiness. I was searching for something that would make me happy. What I discovered is that what we are in search of, be it happiness, love, or peace, is something that has always been there; it's always been ours. But our judgments and opinions would have us believe that we are not good enough, worthy enough, or deserving enough to accept that happiness, that love, that peace. So, we search for it. Once we know who we really are we know exactly what to do.

What makes you happy? What brings you joy? What did you enjoy doing as a child that makes you smile? That's your passion, your calling, and if it happens to be the same as your career, that's wonderful, but if it's not, that's okay because it doesn't have to be. You can fulfill your passion outside of your career.

If you are a right-brain person, as I am, you may also notice that you don't have goals, but you have dreams instead. You tend to trust your intuition, and the journey is more important to you than the goal, and you don't care much about the rules. On the other hand, if you are a left-brain person, it's important for you to have fixed goals, to plan everything, and have a bucket list. Logic comes first, and there is no place for fairy tales in your reality.

From the moment the memories of our true selves began to fade away in early childhood, we have been searching for that connection, the feeling that something is missing in us, that there is something wrong with us. So, we go through life, trying to fill that void with something or someone on the outside. If we feel that love is missing from our life, we search for a partner to fill that void. If being valued or feeling important is missing, we seek success and recognition from the outside world.

What do you think you need in your life right now to be happy? Make the decision to be happy without it, and you will realize that it's all part of the illusion. Everything you need is already within you. Being happy has nothing to do with what's going on out there. Happiness is an inside job. Be the source of happiness, regardless of what is going on around you and regardless of what you have or don't have. I had to let go of limiting beliefs to realize that happiness is not something I deserved, it's something I choose. It's already inside me. Once I removed the masks of the ego, there it was; it's always been there, waiting for me to choose it. Happiness is being present right now in each moment. If you wait until some future event or for something out there to make you happy, you will be miserable. This moment is the only one you have.

It doesn't matter what you believe, just be true to yourself. We are here to discover and express our true identity. "Maybe the journey isn't so much about becoming anything. Maybe it's about unbecoming everything that isn't really you, so you can be who you were meant to be in the first place."[38] - Paulo Coelho. In every moment, act on your highest joy to the best of your ability and without expectation. Keep an open mind and heart, and have an attitude of exploration and curiosity. There is no end to this adventure and many ways to experience it all. We are only limited by our beliefs. Life is meant to be lived here and now; have fun with it. Humans tend to complicate things. If something is complicated, you know it's coming from the ego. Spirit is always simple. Just trust the process as it always evolves, and it is a joyful ride!

---

38 https://www.goodreads.com/author/quotes/16593449.Paul_Coelho

CHAPTER 9

PARALLEL UNIVERSES, OTHER DIMENSIONS, AND DREAMS

Who we are is a consciousness connected to a quantum field of intelligence. We are in it, and it is in us. There are many words used to define this field of intelligence, but they all mean the same thing. It is sometimes referred to as, I am, infinite intelligence, divine intelligence, Tao, God, the creator, source, spirit, life force, the presence, divine light, divine self, higher self, higher consciousness, or infinite consciousness. These are just words to label things, but they are not the thing itself. For example, the word water is not the water. You cannot get wet from the word water. It is the same with the divine. Don't get stuck on words for there really isn't a word for all that is. It doesn't matter what label you use; this field of intelligence is doing everything. Consciousness is the awareness of being, but we do not see the intelligence that runs our program. We can't see it, touch it, or hold on to it, but it operates everything. To use the analogy of the radio or television set, what is operating the programs we hear or see? Even if we looked inside the radio or television, we would not see or touch the electromagnetic waves that operate it, but we can tune in to a frequency and listen to or watch a program.

This divine intelligence is within us all the time, and it responds to who we are. This invisible intelligence is your spirit self, manifesting through your soul, expressing itself through your earthly personality. It exists without the physical body, but without it, the physical body is just a shell. It beats your heart, grows your hair, and animates all life. When this intelligence withdraws, your physical body becomes completely inanimate. Some may think that the physical brain is in control. You can consider the brain as the command center, but it is not the commander. The ghost in the machine is your divine intelligence. It controls all activities of the human body. That part of you cannot be found in an autopsy. That commander inside the body is real, and what is real never changes. The body is constantly changing, and therefore it is not real. The body you had when you were a baby or when you were ten no longer exists. That body has changed, and you cannot bring it back.

We are one with the divine intelligence. It is within you as the perfect picture of the oak tree is in the acorn. The divine pattern of your life is in your superconscious mind. As above, so below, and as below, so above. The human mind is an expression of your being just as you are the expression of the divine intelligence. The cells in your body respond to your will, as all of us, being the cells in the body of the divine intelligence, respond to its will. All consciousness is one, whether it be human, plant, animal, or cell consciousness. All is controlled by divine intelligence, which can organize and direct cells to form various organisms.

You, as a person, are only a physical form containing a human brain, through which spirit can express itself in matter. This consciousness is your consciousness, flowing through your soul, expressing itself on all planes of existence all the way to the physical plane of your human brain, the same way this consciousness finds expression through the unfolding of the rose—as it evolves from the bud to the perfect flower. Everything is in divine order. There are no accidents or coincidences. We have come to know a coincidence as something that fits together accidentally, but coincidence is a mathematical term, said to occur when two expressions show a near equality that has no theoretical explanation. A coincident is two lines or shapes that lie exactly on top of each other. In geometry, two angles that coincide together perfectly are said to be two angles that fit together. There is no need to wonder if only circumstances or events had been different. At the conscious level, you may have forgotten that you signed up for everything that happened and is happening in your life, but every event and every person has given, and is giving, you the opportunity to know the real you.

As an extension of the higher consciousness, the human brain mind serves as an instrument to receive information. The vibration is slowed down to the limited mental capacity of the human brain, so it can inform you about the world of matter. It is in this limited consciousness, the physical self, that you have been thinking of yourself as separate from the infinite consciousness, but it is the same consciousness; it is simply reduced to the human brain's capacity to work with it.

The Illusion of Reality

You are not what you think you are. What you think you are is just a shadow of the real you. Only when we, as humans, become fully conscious of the divine intelligence within us, will we realize that we have been asleep, and all these earthly events and conditions are just a dream from which we will awaken. You are not a human being having a spiritual experience; you are a spiritual being having a human experience. As Eckhart Tolle expresses this idea, "[y]ou are the universe expressing itself as a human for a little while."[39]

Quantum physics is a science of mathematics, more specifically, the science of the small, how things behave at the subatomic level. It is the same mathematics used to create a hologram; therefore,

---

39 https://www.azquotes.com/author/14703-Eckhart_Tolle

it can explain why the universe seems more like a hologram than solid reality. No science has been proven more precise than quantum physics.

The atoms (nucleus and electrons) make up the physical universe, a universe that appears solid and real to us. Atoms are possibilities of consciousness. The entire universe is made from waves of possibilities. In a wave every possible outcome exists, all at the same time. Particles are what become your reality. According to quantum physics, reality doesn't exist until it is observed. When you're not looking, it's a wave of possibilities. When you're looking, it's a particle.

One electron is a quantum, and several electrons are a group of quanta. Quanta are the basic stuff from which the universe is made. The only time quanta manifest as particles is when we look at them. An electron is always a wave until it is observed. When observed, the electron collapses to being a particle with a fixed position in space and time, which is what we consider our physical reality. American physicist Nick Herbert says, "[h]umans can never experience the true texture of quantum reality because everything we touch turns to matter."[40] The fact that when we observe quantum reality it turns to matter, makes it hard to prove that this field exists. As mentioned above, we can't see, touch, or hold on to, the quantum field.

This field exists, in a wave form, outside of space and time. Science and spiritually describe this field of *all that is* as an invisible force that shapes the physical world. Science doesn't know who created it or how it came into existence. Science knows only that nothing makes sense without this force. Although quantum physics seems strange and unfamiliar, it explains natural phenomena. Mathematics is the language of physics, and without mathematics our physical world would be difficult to understand. Albert Einstein once said, "[p]eople like us, who believe in physics, know that the

---

40 https://en.wikiquote.org/wiki/Nick_Herbert_(physicist)

distinction between past, present, and future is only a stubbornly persistent illusion."[41]

According to quantum physics, every moment is happening right now. There is only now. Everything occupies the same space, but each dimension vibrates at a different frequency. Each dimension appears solid and real to those living in it. The things you did last year, last week, or yesterday, no longer exist, except in your mind. This sense of time passing is just an arrangement of memories, whether they are regrets from the past or future anxieties, happening now in your mind.

Each moment appears in a frame that really has no movement, but when each moment is projected in a sequence, we get the illusion of space, time, and motion. This is what happens when each frozen frame of a movie passes through a projector and is then projected on a screen, giving the illusion of motion, the illusion of a physical reality. The experience of time is an illusion, created within this reality. Think of the acronym for TIME as The Infinite Moment Experience. Time is the fabric upon which your life's story is written, defining your history and your probable future. Time gives you an illusion of continuity, all in the never-ending moment of now.

In Brian Greene's video, "Past, present and future coexist. 'Now time' explained easy," he uses the analogy of a loaf of bread. Each slice is a life, parallel to the other slices, but all the slices are part of the same loaf, all lives happening at the same moment. Past and future are just perspectives, different slices of the same loaf, the same now. They are all equally real. They all exist right now. Everything that has ever happened or will happen, all exist. The other parallel universes seem nonexistent because we experience only the reality that is relevant to our state of consciousness. We are focused on this reality.

41 https://www.goodreads.com/author/quotes/9810. Albert_Einstein?page=7

Let's say I see an advertisement for a cruise to the Caribbean. This opens several possibilities of events, depending on what I choose. The first possibility is that I decide to stay home and not to go on the cruise. The second possibility, I decide to go on the cruise to the Caribbean. The third possibility, I decide to go on a cruise, but to Alaska. Once I make a decision and the event happens, what happens to the other probabilities? I observe the event that is happening in this reality, while the others appear to have been eliminated; they have collapsed in this reality, but they could be occurring in parallel universes.

This concept can appear strange to our physical minds, which have a limited view and understanding of the universe. In the example of a radio or a television mentioned earlier, several channels are available on the radio or television, and all channels play music or movies in the same now. They are all equally real; they all exist, but you hear only the one you are tuned in to, on the frequency of the channel you chose. It doesn't make the other stations or channels less real; they are just playing on a different frequency. When you change the channel, the other programs are still running.

Reincarnation

The exploration of past lives provides insight into the possibility and probability of other dimensions and parallel universes.

When in deeper states of consciousness such as meditation, hypnosis, or past-life regression, it is possible to get glimpses of our other selves, who are living in different realms and are vibrating at different frequencies. What we consider memories from different lifetimes could simply be other realities that we are also living at the same moment. Time travel is not so much traveling through time; it is simply shifting frequency. Whether we see a life event as a past life or a parallel life, that moment is an opportunity for us to explore and learn that leads to a deeper knowing of ourselves as a result. If it enhances our physical life in any way, that's what matters.

When we choose to incarnate on earth, we do not bring one hundred percent of our light energy with us. Our physical brain could not handle that level of energy. Our spirit always remains in the presence of God; our soul has experiences that allows it to grow and develop through the personality that is created at the time of incarnation. So, part of our essence always remains in the spirit world where we can reunite with members of our soul group. This also explains how it is possible to see our relatives even though someone may have died several earth years before and may have reincarnated since.

On the one hand, a more advanced soul, who is confident about handling whatever challenges he or she will have on earth, might bring only twenty-five percent of its total capacity for the next life, but the less confident soul might bring seventy percent, just to be on the safe side. Our soul is multidimensional and can experience simultaneous incarnations by splitting fragments of our energy among all incarnations.

When I assisted clients in exploring past lives, they often reported their experience between lifetimes, where they met with their spirit guides and soul groups. This is something I have experienced as well. Once we leave this physical plane, there is a review of the life just lived and an overview of the many lifetimes. When we explore our lives, we see that all the twists and turns have meaning and purpose. These life reviews are not about punishment for what we might have done; they are for self-enlightenment. The information helps with our prelife planning for our next incarnation and the selection of the next body. When we are shown the big picture and the sum of our multiple incarnations, we understand the reasons for the many challenges we chose and the people we chose to do this with. We hold ourselves accountable for our choices and make our selections accordingly for the next incarnation. There is no judgment.

Souls see this time as rehearsal for their role in the next play on earth's stage, and it's exciting. These memories are hidden from our conscious mind when we are born. Our conscious mind is new, it does not reincarnate. Our soul has been in other bodies and has the memories of other lives. If we instantly remembered it all at the conscious level, the memories would be unbearable and overwhelming, and they would make it difficult to focus on what we have chosen to accomplish. To make the experience seem more real, we are given the illusion of time and space to process each step as the plan unfolds. What might have seemed easy in rehearsal might be viewed as a lot more traumatic and dramatic in physical form. I think we perhaps forget, from one life time to the next, how dense the physical world really is. So, it's okay to not take ourselves so seriously and to laugh at the silly messes we get ourselves into along the way. Some part of us thought it was a great idea! In some incarnations, we take on few challenges and just coast through life, but sometimes, we push ourselves to overcome as many challenges as we can handle to further our spiritual growth. I think this is one such lifetime for me—I wanted to check many boxes off my list.

When we plan to experience great challenges, it is with the intent to evolve, not to suffer and become lost. The plan includes ways to overcome the experience. Nothing is as it appears. What the human personality's limited perspective sees as a negative experience, in which someone may appear as a victim, the soul, being aware of the bigger picture, knows the meaning and the reason behind that experience. The personality sees only the tip of the iceberg, while the soul is aware of what is happening below the surface. That's why it's helpful to ask your soul's help to make sense of it all. The soul will provide a much deeper understanding and the ability to see the experience as a blessing. Fear will be replaced with love and judgment will be replaced with respect and admiration because we have a knowing that we bravely agreed to these challenges.

Even though the soul experiences a great amount of healing between incarnations, some healing is possible only while in a physical body. The healing has to be felt, and the earthly personality is the best vehicle for that purpose. Sometimes, when we incarnate, we choose to be in a comedy, and sometimes, we choose to be in a horror movie, depending on what we have decided to overcome or accomplish for our spiritual growth. Due to the limited understanding of the conscious mind, during our time in the physical realm, we believe that we are helpless victims and that we deserve to suffer. In the same way that we agree to sit down and watch a movie, we agree to believe in the movie's reality for the duration of the movie. Just like the actors in the movie, we don't really die or get hurt. Some actors have been together in many films.

This preplanning probably seems like our destiny is set in advance and cannot be changed, but in all our lives, we have the freedom to choose a different fork in the road and so do the other players. We are the writers and producers of our own movies. No major event is set in stone; they are all potential or probable events, and the personality has the option to choose a different path. We can change any scenes or actors that we want to at any time. Depending on what we and other players decide to do, we can alter the plan as certain threads become activated and become real possibilities in this dimension. How do we choose to respond to the plan? We can walk out when we want, or we can watch the same movie over and over. Do we resist it or go through it to heal and grow? Who you are now is the result of all your former choices. Other potential threads of these major life events exist in different dimensions with the other fragments of you. You are an actor playing different roles at the same time, in different movies, on different screens.

How we react to our challenges can eliminate the need for a certain planned experience. If we have already achieved the growth intended, that experience will simply fade away from your time line.

Once a life plan is set in motion, events will occur in which your higher self will influence the possibility of meeting the people you have made agreements with. That's when you get a sense that a sequence of events is meant to be that way.

When we experience déjà-vu moments of having been in a certain place before, knowing full well we've never been there, or having already had a particular conversation with someone, even though you're meeting this person for the first time, these moments could be a past-life/parallel life memory. Or they might simply be a glimpse of the prelife rehearsal that pops into our mind when our spiritual plan and our physical path cross.

I was leading a group regression one day. Twenty-five people were sitting in a circle. After the regression, people shared their experiences. Two of the women, who did not know each other, described the same exact scene. During the regression, they had both found themselves at the same moment in the same past life. And they each described what they saw from their view across the river from where they were sitting. They saw the same people and the same scenes. It was incredible.

Once you experience deeper states of consciousness and become aware that you have consciousness independent of your physical body, you realize that you don't die; you simply transform, and you know that you will meet your loved ones again. Even if we don't understand it completely, there is life beyond this physical dimension. We may not have a physical body, but we choose the form that is best suited for our continued learning and evolution in that dimension.

During some of the psychic readings I have done for people, I have received messages from deceased relatives of the person I was reading for. I will always remember the first time it happened; it was totally unexpected. Within a few minutes of reading for this woman, I started getting messages from her husband, but I had no idea that he had passed. The messages made complete sense to her, so I kept going. In all my previous readings, I had received a clear description of whoever I was seeing, but this time, I said to this woman, "I can't see his physical body." She replied, "[h]e passed away two weeks ago." Well, that caught me by surprise. The channel was open, allowing for clear communication between dimensions, and beautiful messages followed from this man to the spouse he had left behind. Those messages brought so much peace and comfort to this woman. I was truly grateful to have been part of that experience.

The communication didn't stop there. I think the word got around in the spirit world because many other souls who had passed started to see me as a possible channel of communication. Soon, I began to attract people who needed to receive messages from their loved ones. Each reading was a precious moment for me and for everyone involved. A young couple came to my office one day, wanting to communicate with someone. The woman could not stop crying, so I explained to them that I could not promise that a specific individual would show up but that I would do my best to connect with whoever they were supposed to hear from that day. As the reading began, I had difficulty interpreting the messages I received. The departed soul had very few words to say, but he started showing me drawings of specific moments he had had with his mom and dad. He told me that he was two years old when he died. He was the child that the couple had lost just two months before they came to see me. He had reassuring messages and told his mom that she would be pregnant again because he was coming back. This young couple left my office feeling comforted and hopeful. I had to close my practice shortly after that because of the motorcycle accident, so I was not able to keep in contact with them to find out what happened.

Messages of souls returning to a family have come up quite frequently during readings. A friend of ours and his wife came by one day. His wife's mother and sister, who had both passed, joined us. The mother just stayed off in the distance and did not speak, but the sister had a message for them: they would be pregnant the following year, the baby was going to be a girl, and the sister was the one coming back. Since we were connected on social media, I did hear back from them, and yes, they got pregnant the following year, and a baby girl was born.

It has been a sensational and deeply rewarding experience to have been the messenger for everyone who was put on my path. From what I have experienced firsthand, I truly believe that, when we transition from this physical existence, we don't die, we simply transform. As we evolve, we are eventually liberated from reincarnation.

Once I had opened the channel of communication with other realms, during some of the hypnotherapy sessions with clients, I also came across souls whom I would describe as being stuck between realms. They needed help to move on, and I was able to assist. The thoughts and emotions someone is focused on when their physical body dies can greatly affect their transition. We are all greeted when we cross over, but no one forces us to accept what is presented. Some choose to hold onto their thoughts and remain stuck between lives until they decide to let go and follow their guides. It's no different than life in the physical dimension. I encountered souls who were extremely angry at someone at the time of a sudden or tragic death, causing them to attach themselves to the person they were angry at. During sessions with a number of clients, I became aware of the presence of such souls. I would call on the departed soul's spirit guides and mine. Then I acted as a facilitator from this side of the veil, learning about the details of the situation that had transpired. Together, we helped that soul understand what had happened and convinced it to move on. I also encountered souls who were afraid when they first left their body. When that happens, souls will search for a light, which can be the bright aura of someone who is in the room with them at the time, to go to. They just need someone to reassure and guide them. All the souls I have been fortunate to assist in that way have always expressed so much gratitude. It is a very rewarding experience.

Just as the unresolved thoughts and emotions we leave this life with will come back with us to be healed in another incarnation, the thoughts and emotions we hold on to as we fall asleep will be reflected in our dreams.

Dreams

The dream state is another way to communicate with other dimensions. While dreaming, you access a frequency that is different from your physical consciousness, and you experience a different reality, but the you that is sleeping in your bed doesn't go anywhere. Your physical body still exists in the same now moment, but you are experiencing another moment in another dimension that appears real to the you in the dream. At the same time, your physical body does not exist in that reality. Your consciousness, not your personality, is what experiences these other realities. Fred Alan Wolf, an American theoretical physicist, specializing in quantum physics, believes that lucid dreams, in which the dreamer becomes aware that he or she is dreaming, are actually visits to parallel realities.

Every dimension has its own frequency, but they all exist right now. For example, imagine yourself in a boat on a lake. Below you, there is another world going on at the same time that is unaware of your existence. The fish don't know that you exist in this other world above them. They vibrate at a different frequency. It is like another dimension. You are aware of it, and you can glimpse through to it on a clear day, but you cannot be in that dimension with the type of body you have now. You need special equipment to remain in that realm for more than a few minutes—just like the fish cannot live in our realm for more than a few minutes. So, there are probably other beings above our dimension, and we are unaware of their existence. We don't know that they exist in this world above us. They vibrate at a different frequency. It is like another dimension. They are aware of our dimension and can glimpse through to it, but they cannot be in our dimension with the types of body they have or live in our realm for long. We can, perhaps, also glimpse into their realm but cannot live in it with the type of body we have. And within the limitations of our human consciousness, we cannot understand them—even if they were right in front of us, trying to communicate. It would be like us trying to have a conversation with the fish.

The same goes with souls who have left the physical realm. They may try to communicate with us, but we can't hear them unless we get on the same frequency. When we leave the physical plane of existence, leaving the conscious mind behind, the subconscious becomes the functioning mind. This is also what happens when we dream;

the subconscious mind takes over; therefore, it is possible to communicate with someone who is no longer in the physical realm as you are both on the same level of consciousness, the same frequency. When my father passed away, I saw him leave his body with two beings of light by his side. I lived three thousand miles away and didn't know he had passed. When one of my sisters called ten minutes later, I already knew. During the six months following his death, I had frequent dreams in which he shared moments of his life in the realm he was now in. He always appeared to be in his thirties, even though he was ninety when he passed. His life seemed to be a continuation of the things he used to enjoy on earth. Then one day, the dreams stopped; I am sure it was time for him to continue onward with his development, but I know we will meet again. My oldest brother and his wife also appeared in my dreams shortly after they passed. They had messages that they wanted to give to their son and daughter, my niece and nephew. Dreams are one of the best ways for departed souls to reach us.

We often receive messages about what we are currently experiencing in our waking life through dreams. If you remember the dream, write it down when you can, but don't force it or get caught up trying to relive the dream. Just like stories from your childhood or from another lifetime that you may have explored through hypnotherapy or past-life regressions, all these moments happen simultaneously in dimensions that vibrate at different frequencies. The moment your focus is back to your physical reality and changes to a different frequency, the moment from the dream or the other life experience, fades away. But the same guidance system is at work.

Have you noticed how dreams seem to just start in the middle of a situation? They don't seem to have a beginning and an end. There is no need for a story like we need to have in the physical realm. In one instant, we are just in the middle of things without knowing how we got there. We experience what we need to, then the dream's over. The you that is dreaming is the real you.

Images are the language of the subconscious mind. That is how it communicates with you, so it's important to learn the meaning of these images. If there's something in your conscious life that you choose to ignore, it will eventually show up in your dreams. Dreams will help you solve problems and help you prepare for what's ahead. Some dreams may offer a warning, some may offer guidance, others may be precognitive, and sometimes, they will simply be about processing the day you just had.

Since communications from your subconscious mind are like hearing a message in a foreign language, your subconscious will use situations that are happening in your life to relay a message to you as clearly as possible. It can even use a situation from a movie or TV show that you just watched. Except for the actual dream conversations with a departed loved one, every person or prop in your dream represents an aspect of you. When the other person in your dream— your brother or parent, a friend, or a character from the movie— shows up, think about what that person or character represents or means to you. What's the first thought that comes to mind when you think about this person? Does he or she represent someone who is courageous or someone who loves you, or does that person make you angry? The same principle applies to animals; what does that animal represent to you? That is the message you need to hear.

The first thing to do upon awakening is to notice the feeling from the dream; use that to get to the message of the story. Do you feel concerned, scared, or excited? Then write down what actions are taking place in the dream and any other significant details or symbols you remember. For example, if the dream takes place in a house, the condition and the portion of the house have significant meaning. These aspects are usually associated with the physical body or with one's current state of consciousness. Images are personal; therefore, each person is the best interpreter of his or her own symbolism, but you can also find insightful information in books on dream interpretation, such as *The Encyclopedia of Symbolism* by Kevin J. Todeschi, which is very complete and easy to use.

If you have a recurring dream—with the same person, animal, or theme, you haven't understood the message yet, and the dreams will continue and will usually intensify until you get it. When something is hugely exaggerated in the dream, such as the size of an animal, your subconscious mind is really trying to get your attention.

I have given several workshops on dream interpretation, and dreams have been a wonderful guidance system throughout my life. At the time when my life had fallen into a rut and had left me feeling anxious and unfulfilled, recurring dreams indicated that I had lost my way. The dreams were all about having lost my purse and searching endlessly, leaving me feeling anxious and that something important was missing. This is my personal symbolism for having lost my way. Similar dreams had occurred several years earlier, and I recognized the message when they showed up again. That's when I started meditating again, going within to find my way back to my reason for being here, which lead me to writing this book, and fulfilling my true passion.

Here's another example of a time when my subconscious was really trying to get my attention. I was in a job that I really hated, and I sat down with pen and paper, as usual, to process my feelings about this job. This is what I wrote: "I hate my job; I'm wasting my time there. I'm frustrated. I feel stuck, trapped, at someone's mercy." In the two weeks that followed, I had a series of recurring dreams with that particular theme. In the first dream, I was stuck in a very small office with four other people. In the second dream, I was pushing against a door, and trying to lock it to prevent this dangerous person from coming in. I tried to get out of there to be among friendly people to protect me. The third dream was again about being in a panic to lock the door before the dangerous person could get in. In the fourth dream, I stepped into a very small elevator, then noticed that young, white tigers were sleeping in the corners. They woke up, and I realized that I was in the wrong elevator. As I tried to get out, the tiger that was sleeping by the door started to bite me. I felt scared and wanted to get out. My life was in danger, and I needed to find a safer place. A tiger showed up again in the fifth dream. This time it was an adult tiger, trying to get inside the house, and I hurried to close the door, but he was stronger than I am, and got in. I climbed on a sofa, and the tiger was in front of me, trying to grab me.

The theme is the same in all five dreams, and the level of danger keeps increasing each time, going from a dangerous person to young tigers to a full-grown tiger. In dream interpretation, tigers are generally associated with aggression, dominance, and danger, and that is what that animal represents to me. To someone else, a tiger could have a different meaning. So, my subconscious mind was doing its best to get me to pay attention to this feeling of being trapped, of feeling as if I was at someone's mercy, and that it was time to do something about it. It was a message to follow my intuition and take action. The final dream in this series was much different than the others and was preparing me for what was ahead, but I didn't know it at the time. This dream happened in the early hours, just before waking up. Morning dreams are usually about an event in the future, while dreams in the earlier part of the night are more likely to be about a past or current situation. In this last dream of the series, I was in front of a hotel when an enormous wave, as tall as the multistory hotel and like a solid wall of water, appeared out of nowhere, right in front of me. It splashed inland before I could run away and, amazingly, the water flowed back out to sea. I remained untouched and unafraid. I walked to the back of the building and got inside until the storm passed and the sun was shining again.

I took the messages from the dreams into my meditation. I went inside and called on my team of angels to help me get out of that workplace. In meditation, I focused on the vibration of the work environment that I wanted to be in, a loving and joyful place, filled with kindness and laughter, a place where divine harmony is the frequency of the day. I asked for something better.

During that week, I was also experiencing lower back pain. The list of probable feelings that could cause this pain indicated that it was related to feeling unsupported financially, experiencing fear where money is concerned, wanting to back out of something, and running away from a situation. I sure wanted to back out of the choice I had made to accept that job, and I wanted to run away from it as fast as I could.

A few weeks later, in April of 2020, I received a call that terminated my employment because, as a result of the current worldwide pandemic, there was a lack of work. Wow, that was an interesting turn of events. That was not exactly part of my plan. When I asked for help to get out of that work situation, I had no idea this is how it was going to happen. I thought that I could find another job before leaving this one.

Even though I had been through much worse situations than this one, the thought of losing my job created some financial concern. Not knowing how long this crisis was going to last was unsettling, and an old fear pattern tried to show its face. I knew I could find other work, but when, was a question that no one had the answer to. No one was hiring as most businesses were closed. As days turned into weeks, then into months, I had more and more what-if scenarios playing in my mind, and I had to remind myself that losing a job is just a new door opening to a much better opportunity. It required a lot of patience, a lot of trusting the process, and letting things happen while enjoying the ride. Of course, after a few months of sending out several applications, requests for interviews and offers came all at once. I listened to my intuition and turned down the first two offers, since they didn't feel right. I surrendered to the change, remembering one of my favorite sayings, "I put this situation in the hands of infinite love and wisdom. I trust in the divine plan." As discussed in chapter 6, time is not in a straight line; it is a spiral, so you may encounter a situation again, giving you an opportunity to discover its deeper truth.

The best way to find out what you're made of is to face a new challenge. I have definitely had my share of new challenges, which have left me feeling sad, depressed, discouraged, overwhelmed, afraid, lost, frustrated, and confused, but they have not brought me down. I have always bounced back and always will. If you trip and fall down a hill, you sometimes find a beautiful gem that you would have missed had you not fallen.

In the words of Neale Donald Walsch, "the acronym for FEAR is **Feeling Excited And Ready.**"[42] I had a choice. Was I going to let this crisis devastate me or see it as a new opportunity? In the Chinese language, the word crisis is composed of two characters, meaning danger and opportunity. By now, I have learned to let go and trust that everything is happening in divine order. In my unemployment circumstance, I chose opportunity and expressed gratitude for the time off as it would give me the opportunity to finish writing my book. I surrendered to the infinite intelligence in charge and decided to gently row my boat down the stream, and be amazed that everything I needed would appear at exactly the right moment. As that last dream showed me, I would come out of this storm totally fine. I would be safe from this giant wave, all I had to do was go back inside until the storm passed. I went back inside, checked in with my inner self, relaxed, trusted the process, and let things happen. A few weeks later, I received the job offer I wanted.

This is why it's so important to pay attention to the messages you receive, no matter how they show up for you, and write them down, so that you can better understand their meaning. Those dreams about danger were possibly also warning me about the serious condition about to happen in the world.

Write or record your dreams as quickly as you can when you wake up because they will fade away quickly and be forgotten. When you awaken and move out of the subconscious state, a veil drops, and it is difficult for the conscious self to look back through that veil to remember the details of what happened. The conscious self was not the one having the dream. So, write all the details you

---

42 https://spiritlibrary.com/neale-donald-walsch/
but-what-about-fear-whats-exciting-about-that

remember, even if they don't make sense to you at the time. When I reread dreams from previous months, most of the time I don't even remember having them, but when I connect them with other dreams, everything eventually makes sense. When you write dreams down, you can see the message unfold.

Have you ever awakened from a dream, and thought, "[t]hat was interesting"? So, perhaps when we leave this life experience, this story, and wake up in a different dimension, what we understand as death, we will also say, "[t]hat was interesting!" To quote American-British poet, T.S. Eliot, "[w]e shall not cease from exploration. And the end of all our exploring will be to arrive where we started and know the place for the first time."[43] Death is simply the end of one experience and the beginning of another, like walking through a door into another room. To us, here in this realm, death is an absolute mystery. Death does not exist in the sense that everything is energy and energy never dies. It is simply transformed. Time and space cease to have any meaning, and what dies is the personality, the human identity. Life and death are an inseparable continuum. This divine energy is like an unending ocean. When some of its water is poured into a human vessel, it is confined and limited to that body, but it's still the same water. At the death of the physical body, the water returns to the vast ocean. There is nothing to be afraid of, the only thing you will discover in other realms is more of yourself.

Seven Planes of Existence

According to Eastern philosophy, the universe has seven planes of existence that are all connected and interconnected. These seven planes are known under various names, depending on who you ask, but the concept is the same. Each has its own frequency or vibration; the earth plane has the slowest vibration, which makes it possible

43 https://www.goodreads.com/quotes/644987-we-shall-not-cease-from-exploration-and-the-end-of

for us to observe matter. To use the example of a ceiling fan, at its slowest speed, you can easily see each individual blade, but with increasing speed, the blades are no longer visible, even though they are still there. Similarly, the vibrations increase with each plane, and we experience different realms of existence, perhaps living several lives simultaneously, because we exist at all levels. When we are here in a physical body, only a small percentage of our soul is inside the body. Another percentage can be in a parallel life, and part of our essence always remains with our source.

These realms are not places that exist in linear time somewhere. They vibrate around us all the time, but to help us understand their meaning at this level of consciousness, we could compare them to the steps of a ladder. We can only see what exists on the steps below us; we do not have access to what is above us until we graduate to that level—when we have attuned to the proper frequency. Or to use the analogy of a building with the ground floor being the physical plane, as you move up to higher floors, the perspective is entirely different.

Each plane is divided by a thin veil. The first plane is the Physical Plane, known as the earth plane, where we currently exist. It is the densest of the seven planes.

The second plane is the Etheric Plane or Lower Astral Plane. The etheric body is the closest to the physical body and the first step to connect you to the universe. You step into that body when you are dreaming or having an out-of-body experience. This plane of existence is a place of rejuvenation. It looks like your physical body, so it feels familiar to your consciousness when you enter the spirit world. This level can also be accessed during meditation.

The third plane is the Upper Astral Plane. This is where our consciousness is focused between lifetimes, when we are between physical bodies. It is believed that we all go through this Astral Plane when we die, to evaluate the last life and to prepare for the next earthly incarnation.

The fourth plane is the Causal Plane, known as the mental plane. It is made purely of thought. This is where our mind time travels, where our thoughts go to the past or future.

The fifth plane is the Akashic Plane where the records of everything that happens in the universe exist. This is the central plane that interconnects the other six realms. Akashic, is a Sanskrit word meaning outside of space and time. It is the information realm, much like the Internet, to which you can connect instantly and access information. It is encrypted for your own protection, and you will be shown only what you are ready to see.

The sixth plane is the Buddhic Plane, the realm of souls who have achieved physical communication with the Tao, such as Jesus and Buddha. This realm creates the laws of the fabric of the universe—the Law of Magnetism, the Law of Gravity, and the Law of Time.

The seventh plane is the Tao, the way, the universal creative force. It creates all the other planes. It is truth and divinity; it is the realization of being one with all that is—God.

The Seven Levels of the Soul

There are seven levels of evolution of the soul; the first five manifest in the physical plane. The age of the soul can be determined by how it perceives itself and the world around it, depending on how a soul grows during each level. A soul at one level or another is not better or worse, further ahead or behind any other. Remember, just like the roller-coaster example in chapter 7, we're all at a different point of the ride. Some are in front or behind or upside down. Souls move through their own experiences at their own pace in each cycle. If you compare the soul levels to our system of learning, the infant soul is in kindergarten, the baby soul is in elementary school, the young soul is in high school, the mature soul is in college, and the old soul is out in the world. You would not say that someone in elementary school is better or worse than someone in college, for example.

Understanding the characteristics of each level can be helpful in knowing yourself better and can be beneficial in your relationships and interactions with others. Here are the seven levels as described in the book *Messages from Michael* by Chelsea Quinn Yarbro[44]:

The first level is referred to as the infant soul. It sees the world as *me* and *not me*. The infant soul goes through life with a "[l]et's not do it" attitude. It sees the world as a fearful place, is inclined to act violently, and sees love in the form of lust. It has no interest in getting a higher education.

The second level is referred to as the baby soul. It sees the world as *me* and *many other me's*. The baby soul goes through life with a "[d]o it right or not at all" attitude. The baby soul believes in the forces of evil and in what others around it believe, and lives by standard cliches. To the baby soul, sexuality is shameful. The baby soul sometimes seeks higher education.

The third level is referred to as the young soul. It sees the world as *me* and *you* as different from *me*, and wants to change you to its point of view. It goes through life with a "[d]o it my way" attitude. The young soul is very attached to the physical body. It is a go-getter, and usually seeks higher education. The young soul can take its beliefs to extremes, either being religiously inclined or atheistic. It can perceive sex as evil and something to be avoided, or it can go to the other extreme and embrace total sexual freedom.

The fourth level is referred to as the mature soul. It sees others as they see themselves. It goes through life with a "[d]o it anyplace but here" attitude. It seeks meaningful loving relationships. It always seeks higher education, but not necessarily in conventional establishments. Focus is on introspection and religion takes a more spiritual path as the mature soul begins to search for truth. It senses the veil between dimensions and seeks to get a glimpse of what lies beyond.

---

44 Quinn Yarbro, Chelsea. Messages from Michael. London: Penguin Publishing Group, 1995 (first published 1979)

The mature soul is sensitive to negative vibrations and prefers to surround itself with peaceful souls.

The fifth level is referred to as the old soul. It is aware that we are all part of something greater. It goes through life with a "[y]ou do what you want to, and I'll do what I want" attitude. The old soul searches intensely and is driven toward spiritual evolution. It is aware of the games of the ego personality. The old soul may or may not be inclined to obtain higher education; it prefers to work in an easy, non-stressful environment, leaving time and energy to pursue its real goals. The old soul sees sex as having no purpose and begins to lose interest. Religion has become about being in nature, in harmony with other creatures. Animals, even wild animals, respond naturally to the old soul. The old soul is intently driven to reunite with its source, and may perceive the presence of realized masters. A longing to return home can at times manifest as depression.

The sixth level is referred to as the transcendental soul. At this level the soul is not in physical form, unless its presence is required to give rise to an imperative spiritual, philosophical, or cultural revolution. It can choose to enter the physical realm by displacing an old soul to fulfill that requirement. Organized religion is of no interest to the transcendent soul. Socrates, Mohammed, and Gandhi are examples of Transcendental Souls.

The seventh level is referred to as the infinite soul. Like the transcendental soul, the infinite soul is not in physical form, unless its presence is needed. The infinite soul perceives the Tao, "the way" and has access to all knowledge of creation. The infinite soul does not incarnate to lead the army; it comes to deliver the word of God, leaving it up to us to listen and take initiative. Jesus, Krishna, and Lao-Tzu are examples of Infinite Souls.

CHAPTER 10

ANGELS, GUIDES, AND MASTERS

There are invisible beings who help us all the time. They are sometimes referred to as angels or spirit guides who come near our energy field to inspire us. Not all souls choose to incarnate in this physical dimension. Spirit guides are souls who have incarnated in the physical realm, angels have not. Just like we have a family here on earth, we also have a spirit family. They are our team, ready to guide and assist us in making choices. Guides have different areas of expertise, so different ones will show up in our lives depending on what we need. We seem to be more aware of these energies when we are young. From the time we are born to about age seven, we still function mostly at the subconscious level of awareness, as the veil between levels of consciousness is much thinner. Young children often talk about their imaginary friends. This is not just fantasy; they are most likely aware of beings in other realms. We are all connected to a universal consciousness and can therefore receive guidance and support from all beings.

We share many lifetimes with our family members, in different roles, as they are part of our soul group. Between lifetimes, we can serve as spirit guides to those in physical form. So, it is possible for a relative who has passed to show up as one of your spirit guides.

However, just because someone has passed, it doesn't mean that they become instantly wise and have all the answers. If you would not have taken advice from your Uncle Charlie when he was alive, why would you want to take advice from him after he passed? Just because he now exists in a different dimension does not necessarily make him more enlightened than you. The same way we continue to grow and evolve in the earth plane, our growth continues once we cross over to another realm. We become more aware, but not necessarily more evolved and all knowing the moment we leave our physical body. As discussed in the previous chapter, depending on where one is on the ladder, one can see only the levels below, not the ones above. So, Uncle Charlie could give you insights from his point of view of whatever is below him, but he does not necessarily have access to all the other higher levels.

Be mindful of your intention when asking for guidance, and be aware of whom you're listening to. This advice applies to the physical as well as the spiritual realm. If you let your ego get in the way, you will attract entities that match your vibration, and not everyone has your best interest at heart. Your spirit guides want you to be the best you possible. When you receive messages from your guides or angels, do not become dependent on your guides or angels. You are connected to the same source, so trust your own inner wisdom. At times, we all need help from an outside source, and it's perfectly fine to get help from someone to facilitate communication with your guides, but do not become dependent on that person either. I've enjoyed doing psychic readings for people, and I have had people become so dependent on me that they would not make any decisions without having a reading first. It's important to trust your own guidance because the more you do, the better the communication with your inner wisdom will get. Psychic readings should be used as road maps to guide you, but remember that nothing is set in stone; there exists a web of possibilities, and your free will to make different choices can change the course of events.

Human beings have become quite infatuated with the possibility of communicating with beings from other realms. To make it easier for our human intellect to understand, we personalize them, we imagine the qualities such beings must have, and then we believe that they have all the answers to guide us through our human lives. When faced with human problems, we sometimes think we need a master, in spirit or physical form, to bring us the advice we are looking for. We want that being to show up in our lives and to play the part of master or guide, and we just want to obey their instructions. They may bring wonderful wisdom, but they are not masters. Although they may be at a different level than you, they are still a personality. There are several levels of existence with different levels of awareness, which we do not fully understand at the physical level. Angels or guides from higher dimensions do not have personalities.

Those who claim to be masters might be more awakened to other realms of consciousness, perform amazing things, and can certainly provide wisdom and guidance, but they are also still personalities like yourself. When divine beings come into your life, you will not recognize or know them as such at the human level of consciousness as they will not call themselves masters. Highly evolved divine beings do not call themselves masters; instead, they will lead you to discover and remember that the only master is your divine self that is within you.

Astrology

Astrology is a great tool in the sense that it is also a road map for your soul journey during this incarnation. I'm not talking about reading your horoscope to find out if you will meet Mister Right or if you'll be going on a trip. I'm talking about the alignment of the planets at the time of your entrance into this realm and their influence in your life. It's like a snapshot of the universe taken at the moment of your birth. This map will help you understand who you are and what you've come here to do. It is a portrait of you. It will show you patterns from past incarnations and what possibilities and directions exist for the current one.

Each zodiac sign is categorized under one of the four elements—earth, water, fire, and air. Each element has positive and negative traits that our personality can work through to evolve. Capricorn, Taurus, and Virgo are earth signs. Pisces, Cancer, and Scorpio are water signs. Aries, Leo, and Sagittarius are fire signs. Aquarius, Gemini, and Libra are air signs. The constellation the sun was in when you were born determines your zodiac sign, also known as your sun sign. It is your identity. It influences how you go through life and how your ego relates to what shows up. It guides your actions. The constellation the moon was in when your were born is known as your moon sign. It is just as significant as your sun sign. Your moon sign is all about your emotions and how you process feelings. It influences the deeper, hidden parts of yourself. The planet on the eastern horizon when you were born, defined as your rising sign, is your personality. It determines how you appear and present yourself and how you relate to others.

In an astrology chart, you will also find your south and north nodes that show what the soul has come back to learn. They work together so you can become the person you are destined to be. The south node shows what you brought into this life that must be overcome, such as depression, anxiety, anger, or sadness. The north node will guide you to your life's purpose or destiny.

The planets also rule the twelve houses of your birth chart. Each house represents a different area of your life.

The first house, ruled by your rising sign, represents the ego, the self.

The second house represents material possessions.

The third house represents communication.

The fourth house represents home and family.

The fifth house represents romance and creativity.

The sixth house represents health and work.

The seventh house represents marriage and partnerships.

The eighth house represents transformation and regeneration.

The ninth house represents travel and exploration of the higher mind.

The tenth house represents career or profession.

The eleventh house represents hopes, aspirations, and friendships.

The twelfth house represents the collective unconscious and psychic abilities.

Charts contain a great deal more information. I've only mentioned the basic details to demonstrate their usefulness. I had a professional astrology chart done several years ago, which showed strong Saturn and Uranus influences. Looking back, here is how these influences played out in my life so far.

The Saturn influence represents a time to grow up, adolescence is over, and that this growth would most likely show up between the ages of twenty-eight to thirty-two and at fifty-eight. When I was thirty-two, I moved to another country. I knew this would not sit well with my mother, but it was time to spread my wings and begin a new adventure. When I was fifty-eight, I stopped dating and going out to clubs as I had been doing since divorcing and returning to Canada four years previous. As discussed in chapter 3, socializing and dating had occupied most of my weekends, but I lost interest and just wanted to be alone. I had felt like a teenager, and now it was time to grow up.

The Uranus influence in my chart represents breaking the rules and coloring outside the lines, having a 'Wait, is this all there is' attitude. This influence is destined to occur at the age of forty-two. The Uranus influence also indicates that it is time to wake up and live your own authentic life, not the one chosen by your parents or employer. This influence to live my own authentic life would most likely show up at the ages of twenty-one, sixty-three, and eighty-four.

I definitely felt the influence of wanting to break the rules and color outside the lines in my early forties. Thoughts of leaving my twenty-some-year marriage were weighing heavily on my mind then. I wanted to break a major rule, to get a divorce, and stop trying to always be perfect, and allow myself to color outside the lines. The most consuming question during those years was definitely, "wait, is this all there is?" When I was forty-four, I finally broke the rules by divorcing my first husband, moving in with the man who became my second husband, and becoming a certified hypnotherapist.

On time to wake up and live your own authentic life, not the one chosen by your parents or employer at the age of twenty-one, sixty-three, and eighty-four, I would say that in my early twenties, I woke up and knew it was time to live my own authentic life, not the one chosen by my parents or employer. I had become a schoolteacher at the age of eighteen. It had been the obvious choice to follow in the footsteps of my sisters. By the time I was twenty-four, I knew this work was not what I wanted to do for the rest of my life, and I quit. At the time of writing this chapter, I am sixty-two and going through major changes. It is again time to wake up and live my own authentic life. As for the age of eighty-four, we'll have to wait and see what new adventure shows up then.

Numerology

A great companion to astrology is numerology. Numerology is an ancient system that was used for thousands of years in ancient Egypt and Babylon, in Greece, Rome, China, and Japan. It is the mystical study of numbers. Modern Western numerology is most frequently based on the teachings of the Greek philosopher Pythagoras who lived more than 2,500 years ago and who became the father of numerology. He was a brilliant philosopher and mathematician with a passion and fascination with numbers. It is said that he believed that the universe was built on the power of numbers and that everything could be translated to numerical form. Pythagoras assigned a particular number to each letter of the alphabet.

Since numerology explains the relationship between numbers and their mystical nature on both an individual and universal level, it adds another degree of understanding your sign and understanding your place in the world. Like your astrological chart, numerology can act as a self-discovery guide to reveal your strengths and weaknesses as you go through this incarnation, and it can point you in the right direction.

The significance of numbers plays a major role in the understanding of all the world's scriptures. Take the number seven for example, which is considered the number of spiritual perfection. There are seven days in the week, seven colors in the spectrum, seven seals and trumpets in Revelation, and seven candles in the menorah. If you look at the number twenty-two, you find twenty-two chapters in Revelation and twenty-two letters in the Hebrew alphabet, which represent the twenty-two steps and twenty-two paths that the soul has to take to be reunited with all the levels of consciousness.

The Torah, which is the first five books of the Hebrew Bible or of the Old Testament, was written in a form of shorthand, without vowels, and each letter is also a number. It is believed to be the template for the creation of the world; in essence, it reveals the mind of God.

When using numerology, you will begin to notice the synchronicity of events, especially when recurring digits start to show up in your life. The more you pay attention to numbers in your daily life, the more patterns will begin to develop as guideposts. Whenever you are looking for answers to a decision you have to make, your number patterns may appear as a way to validate that you are on the right track.

It is also quite fascinating when you assign the corresponding number to each letter of the alphabet. For example, take the letters of the Hebrew alphabet for God (YHVH), assign the corresponding numbers to each one, then add them together to get the total of twenty-six. The number twenty-six is considered to be the divine signature.

YOD: tenth letter

HE: fifth letter

VAV: sixth letter

HE: fifth letter

If you take the letters of the English alphabet for God, G is the seventh letter, O is the fifteenth letter and D is the fourth letter. The total is also twenty-six.

Significant events in my life have happened in conjunction with the number twenty-six. My father passed away on the twenty-sixth of December. I had the near fatal motorcycle accident on the twenty-sixth of December, seven years later. I started my spiritual journey when I was twenty-six years old. When that number shows up in my life, I pay attention because it has become significant for me. Events in connection with the number twenty-six are validation from my higher self, a divine signature, that my life is unfolding exactly as intended, and that the wisdom associated with each event is what I came here to remember and integrate this time around. When I'm concerned about a situation or a decision I have to make, and the number twenty-six shows up within a few hours or a few days, I know that I'm heading in the right direction and should move forward with the next step.

For some of you, it might be the number eleven, for example. These numbers can show up in two or more recurring digits. It could be the time on your computer indicating 1:11 just as you were concerned about something and wondering if your decision was the best one for you right now. It could be the numbers on a building or a door or on the license plate of the car in front of you. Note what you are doing or thinking about at the moment these numbers appear. The appearance of your significant numbers will validate what you were just wondering about, letting you know that you are on the right track. They provide a confirmation from your inner guidance.

Tarot and Oracle Cards

Another way to get answers to your questions is with cards such as tarot and oracle cards. Tarot and oracle cards have common themes, but oracle cards are different in the sense that they are created by an individual, and tarot is a structured system of archetypal images. Tarot is said to have originated out of ancient Egypt.

The images on the cards help facilitate a dialogue with your own inner wisdom. It is one way to talk to the divine. You can have a professional reading done, or you can do your own minireading by simply asking your question, shuffling the deck, then picking a card. The card you choose will reveal a message for you. Don't analyze with your left brain, just notice the first thought or feeling that comes to your mind. It may seem like you just imagined the thought or feeling that came up, and that is perfectly fine because the images are coming from the right side of your brain. Trust what you receive, and eventually, you will develop your own internal language. If you need more clarification, you can pick a second card.

I have done many psychic readings for people over the years. When I was twenty-six years old (yes, there's that magic number again), I met a woman who became my mentor. Her name was Barbara. I was working at a radio station at the time. She was a clairvoyant who had been invited to do a call-in psychic show. The moment that Barbara and I met, we had an instant connection. She recognized something in me that I didn't know was there. We kept in touch, and she invited me to her house a few months later. When I arrived, I was introduced to a friend of hers who had just stopped by for a visit. Barbara gifted me with a deck of tarot cards, then said, "I want you to do a reading for my friend." "What do you mean?" I replied. I had no idea how to do a reading. She suggested that I should not read any manual on how to read cards, but simply allow my subconscious mind to interpret the images, then relay the messages as I received them, without analysis. Which is exactly what I did, and my first psychic reading happened. It's amazing what you're capable of when you get out of your own way. I have followed her advice and have never read a manual on how to read tarot cards, and I don't plan to. The cards are simply a focus point for me and a way to communicate with my subconscious mind to receive information and messages. I'm not saying that you shouldn't read a manual on card reading; there are no rules, do what works for you.

Before I met Barbara, I had been such a shy person, but everything changed that day. An important part of me, which had been dormant, was awakened. I was able to see what Barbara had seen in me. They say, "[w]hen the student is ready, the teacher appears." Well, I guess I was ready. I am extremely grateful that a wonderful guide like Barbara was put on my path. But our relationship didn't end with a single reading in her home. She also had me accompany her to do a live television show in Toronto where the two of us answered questions from callers. Talk about being stretched way out of my comfort zone! A few months later, she invited me to be a reader at a three-day psychic fair at Toronto's Exhibition Place. That weekend, I did sixty readings. A whole new dimension had been opened.

Palmistry

Pythagoras wrote about handreading as far back as 497 BC. Similar to astrology, your palms contain a map that tells the story of your life and destiny. Each part of the hand corresponds to one of the planets.

In scientific palmistry, the shape and formation of your hands reveal the various aspects of your life and personality. Palmistry is a vast subject, and I will only mention the basic aspects here. The hand that you write with is generally considered to be your dominant or major hand. The minor hand will show you what you were born with. The major hand will show how you adapt to the circumstances of your life. So, if you are right-handed, your left hand indicates what you came with, and your right hand indicates what you do with it. As events occur in your life, data gets recorded on the lines of your hands, so these lines can and do change through the years.

The shape and size of your hands have specific meanings. A square hand signifies practicality, while a long, narrow hand denotes someone with an artistic disposition. If veins are highly visible on the back of the hands, the person is sensitive. The tougher, less sensitive type will have no veins showing. Short fingers represent physical energy, while long fingers signify a reflective personality. The individual with square-shaped fingertips has a practical nature. Rounded fingertips represent sociability. The sensitive and artistic types will have pointed fingertips.

The numerous lines in your palms define many aspects of your life. The three main lines are the life line, the head line, and the heart line. The life line shows how you live; the head line shows how you think and work; and the heart line shows how you feel. The life line starts between your thumb and index finger and bows down toward your wrist. The head line also starts between your thumb and index finger and travels across the hand, in a straight, sloping or curved line. The heart line starts at the edge of the hand and generally curves up between the index and the middle finger, but can also go straight across to the other side. Generally speaking, strong, deep lines show strength and health; weak or fine lines show a nervous disposition or weak health.

Auras and Chakras

An aura is the electromagnetic field that surrounds you. Since everything is energy, every organism and object in the universe radiates an aura. In religious art, auras are depicted as a halo around the head of saints and angelic beings. It would seem that their auras were so powerful that they could be seen or sensed by those around them.

The aura consists of seven levels, each having its own frequency. Each layer of your aura is said to correspond to a different chakra. Auras are around your physical body, and chakras are inside it. The word chakra, meaning spinning wheel, is derived from the Sanskrit language. This energy force, known as the kundalini in the Eastern world, is coiled like a serpent at the bottom of your spine and flows up and down the central nervous system. It is always on, keeping you connected to the universe. The symbology of serpents with wings in ancient Egyptian and Mayan art, represents the kundalini energy being raised to higher consciousness. As well, the story of the fall of the serpent in the Garden of Eden is symbolic of the descent of higher consciousness or life force into the physical realm.

Each chakra is like a power station that distributes etheric energy throughout the body. There are seven main chakras, which are located from the base of the spine to the top of the head, and they are associated with endocrine glands and major organs. They each vibrate to a specific color, like those in a rainbow.

The first chakra, the root chakra, is located at the base of the spine. It is associated with the testes in males and the ovaries in females, and it vibrates to the color red. It connects you to the earth, makes you feel grounded, and gives you a sense of belonging.

The second chakra, the navel or sacral chakra, is located just below your navel. It is associated with the Leydig cells, and it vibrates to the color orange. It relates to the balance between the masculine and feminine energies within each individual. This is the center of sexuality and creativity.

The third chakra, the solar plexus chakra, is located in your solar plexus. It is associated with the adrenal glands, which include the pancreas, spleen, and liver. It vibrates to the color yellow. It is the center of emotions, wisdom, and power. When this chakra is in balance, we experience courage, but when out of balance, we experience fear or resentment.

The fourth chakra, the heart chakra, is associated with the thymus gland, and it vibrates to the color green. This is the midpoint between the three lower centers and the three higher centers, the bridge between heaven and earth. It is the center of love. When this chakra is in balance, we experience love, but when out of balance we experience jealousy and worry.

The fifth chakra, the throat chakra, is associated with the thyroid gland, and it vibrates to the color blue. It is the seat of free will and the center of communication and self-expression.

The sixth chakra, the third eye chakra, is associated with the pituitary gland. It is located at the center of your forehead, between your eyes, and it vibrates to the color indigo. It is the center of inner vision, insight, and awareness.

The seventh chakra, the crown chakra, is associated with the pineal gland. It is located at the top of your head, and it vibrates to the color violet. This is the center of connection to the divine.

Most of today's books represent the chakras in the previously explained way. They teach that the kundalini culminates at the crown chakra, but the ancient scriptures show that the third eye is the highest spiritual center. The energy flows up the spine to the top of your head, unites with source, then flows down to your forehead and into your third eye. In this teaching, the sixth chakra is the crown and the seventh chakra is the third eye. This shape is also represented by the shepherd's staff in Hebrew and Christian mysticism. When I started visualizing the energy flow that way, it seemed more natural to me, and I noticed a significant difference. The vibration in my third eye became much stronger. Try it and see which way resonates best with you. There is no right way or wrong way; it all works.

The chakras are where the physical, mental, and spiritual come together. Negative thinking and suppressed emotions can block the associated chakra and leave you feeling out of balance. For example, if you are hurt in a relationship, your heart center will close up. Memories are stored in clusters of similar emotions, and when emotions get stuck, they block the flow of energy. The more we let go, the easier it is for the energy to flow freely again and to return to a balanced state.

While the colors of the aura change to reveal information about your thoughts and emotions, the colors of the chakras remain constant. Your physical, emotional, and spiritual health will be reflected in the colors of your aura; therefore, it will never be just one color. It will be a mixture of colors and will vary from lighter to darker shades, reflecting your current emotional state.

The spectrum of colors in your aura will change depending on your current state of mind, but the one or two colors closest to your body tend to remain the same. These colors represent your main personality type.

I had an aura chakra analysis done several years ago. The equipment used in such an analysis measures your biodata through biofeedback sensors. This data is then analyzed to provide you a report that gives you a clear representation of your personality type and traits. It will show you how the energy is vibrating in each chakra. Is it low or high? It will show you which areas of your mind and body are balanced or unbalanced. It will reveal what careers would be most fulfilling, which relationships are best for you, your strengths and weaknesses, and more. It will also give you the size of your aura, which indicates how much energy you radiate around you. It's the closest thing to having a *how to* manual for your life.

You have most likely sensed a person's aura. Have you ever noticed how, sometimes, when you meet someone you feel automatically attracted to that individual or are completely turned off? If you've ever felt something strange about someone and didn't quite know what it was, you were picking up the vibration from their aura. It can sometimes be a soul memory of another lifetime with that person as everything is recorded in this electromagnetic field. Listen to your body; it is your vehicle, an amazing instrument in the physical realm.

We have been given tools and maps for our journey. The universe communicates with us through dreams, meditation, numbers, songs, billboards, and even animals. Animals that show up in your waking life at specific moments are also very significant. Each one has a symbolic meaning, and you will develop your own personal meaning as well. Notice what you are focusing on when the animal appears, receive the message, then you will begin to develop your own personal meaning and message each time that animal shows up.

One of my favorite animals is the butterfly. My personal meaning for butterflies is total freedom, growth, and transformation. When they cross my path, the message is to lighten up and stop taking myself so seriously. Many butterflies have crossed my path at the perfect times—as gentle reminders.

The caterpillar, however, means that everything happens in stages, taking small steps, one at a time. One crossed right in front of my foot not long ago as I was out walking and thinking about my next steps in finding the right source of income. During that week, there were also crows cawing in the trees below my balcony for two whole days. And I have not seen many crows during my six years living in this apartment. Crows mean that change is coming, and a future event is calling your attention. Following that, there were doves all around for the next few days, a few of them landed on my balcony and stayed awhile. Doves signify peace, regardless of external circumstances. When a dove flies into your life, you are being asked to go within, listen to your intuition, and trust your divine guidance.

Messages from the universe come in so many ways. They are all around us all the time. The more you pay attention and as you develop your own meaningful symbols, the easier the communication will become. Someone once told me that when a dragonfly shows up in her life, she knows it's a message from her mother on the other side.

Even the fairy tales we are all familiar with have metaphysical interpretations. They are stories of our human development, our separation and reunion with the divine. Take the story of Snow White and the Seven Dwarfs for example. The cruel stepmother symbolizes the negative thoughts that are stored in your subconscious mind. The friendly animals and birds symbolize your intuition. The seven dwarfs represent the protective forces around you, and Prince Charming represents the divine plan for your life. When the prince wakes you up, you live happily ever after. Encoded spiritual messages appear in nearly all fairy tales. They attempt to help us see truth at a deeper level—that we can never be permanently separated from the divine. We are shown the struggle between good and evil and that the curse must be lifted, so we can live happily ever after by reuniting with the divine.

The Tree of Life

The Tree of Life is the primary image of one of the most ancient of all mystery traditions, the mystical Qabala. The treasures of the universe, how it was formed, and how we are the product of divine energy that has densified into physical matter are portrayed in the powerful symbolism of the tree.

The Tree of Life is also a map that guides us within to find answers. It includes astrology, numerology, tarot, and mythology. As previously discussed, symbols and images are the way the subconscious mind communicates with the conscious mind. So, it is with the symbols and images of the Tree of Life; they are tools to help us open doors to levels of consciousness beyond our normal waking consciousness, guiding us to find solutions to our problems.

The Tree of Life consists of ten sephiroth or levels of consciousness. Each sephira represents a level of the subconscious mind. There are seven bottom levels and three higher, more abstract levels. Each level corresponds to the chakras of the human body. The twenty-two paths of wisdom mentioned earlier are used to assist in our development toward expanded awareness. The images and symbols of the tree reveal to us who we are, why we are here at this time, and what we have come to accomplish. When using the numerology of your birthdate in correlation with the tree, you also discover your strengths and weaknesses.

After studying the Qabala, I understood the advice I had received from my mentor Barbara about doing tarot card readings. By focusing upon the images and symbols on the cards, I became opened to the subconscious energies and could interpret the received messages.

The tree itself is an ancient symbol of life, growth and change, leaves falling and reappearing season after season, dying only to be reborn. Its roots are grounded in the earth, and it reaches to the sky. Trees play an important role in human lives on so many levels. You have most likely used the expression *knock on wood* on several occasions as a way to avoid misfortune and to allow your lucky streak to continue. This action started as a practice to make sure that there were no spirits in the tree before it was cut down.

The universal, archetypal symbol of the cross is also a representation of the Tree of Life. It is the communication between heaven and earth, the vertical line being the spiritual plane, and the horizontal line, the physical plane. The cross represents the spiritual manifesting in the physical and is a symbol of man's harmonious expansion on both planes.

We are provided with many tools and assistance when we incarnate into this realm, which we discover when we are ready.

EPILOGUE

Yesterday I was clever, so I wanted to change the world.
Today I am wise, so I am changing myself.[45] — Rumi

Life is a series of adventures. I brought something back from each adventure, and this book has allowed me to share with you the gems of wisdom I have unearthed. I hope that sharing my story will have a positive influence in the life of whomever has been drawn to this book.

We have the tools and a map; we can do this! Observe yourself from a larger perspective. Be like the astronaut who leaves the earth as a scientist, and comes back as a mystic after seeing the earth from a broader viewpoint.

By looking at our beliefs and the circumstances that helped shaped those beliefs, we can get a better understanding of our pre-birth plan, to remember who we are and why we're here. Look at the culture, the religion, the family you were born into, and make note of the key players of the major events in your life. There was a mutual agreement for growth with all the characters who were or are now part of your life experience.

I made agreements with key players who would help me over-come the fear of abandonment, fear of not being loved, sadness, fear of having done something wrong, fear and resentment of being

---

45 https://wisdomquotes.com/rumi-quotes/

controlled. Through all these circumstances, I would learn to become independent, courageous, and happy.

My religious beliefs were formed early on from a Catholic upbringing. I chose an emotionally absent mother, whose strong beliefs were opposite of mine, and, to balance things out, a father who was loving and accepting. Through my interactions with them, I experienced the fear of being abandoned by my caretakers, being left behind, and losing someone I love. You see, in my past lives and prelife explorations, I discovered that they had been my parents before. Then they had been forced to give me away to a more financially stable family. My father played a key role in teaching me love and acceptance of myself and others without judgment.

The fear of being abandoned and losing someone I love was definitely something I chose to overcome in this lifetime. It was the theme of my experience with my second husband, which was left over from a previous life together. If we have unfinished business, we will see recurring patterns in our lives.

Being raised in the Catholic religion was a perfect way to experience the fear that I've done something wrong, that I'm unworthy and unlovable. My mother and my first husband, both being emotionally absent, played their roles, showing me that I was holding on to this feeling of being unlovable and the sadness that resulted from it.

The fear of being controlled was also a recurring theme that my mother played a role in. My mother was the type of person who preferred to have people behave in a way that she thought was best, and I resented being controlled. I wanted to do things my way and did not agree with her beliefs. The same pattern continued with my first husband. He wanted to decide and control everything I did until the end of our marriage, and I eventually resented that behavior. Having felt controlled my entire life, I then tried to control my husband in my second marriage, and he became resentful. Having experienced both sides of this behavior and having evolved from it, this pattern will most likely not repeat itself in my future lifetimes.

Since we learn from contrast, fear had to be present in my experiences so I could choose to be courageous. All the times I was afraid, I could have succumbed to the fear and decided not to follow my plan of learning courage—the courage to be independent and be okay by myself, the courage to realize that I am the source of my happiness. This was a major accomplishment for me, and I'm grateful to all the players who acted their roles perfectly.

I apparently needed some hard lessons to overcome the behavior of always wanting to please, being unable to say no, and afraid of disappointing. Two of these lessons almost ended my current life experience. Over time, I had lost my sense of self-worth and was afraid to share my opinions and feelings. By learning to trust my feelings and my intuition, I continue to elevate my vibration and bring my male and female energies in perfect balance, and I'm stronger for it.

In all circumstances, I could have blamed the other players and held them responsible, but I would have continued to attract more similar situations in my life. I chose to evolve. What are the themes and patterns of your life story, and who are the main characters who have agreed to share the stage with you?

Live as a witness to your own life. Step out of the illusion and observe. Everything that happens to you is created for your spiritual evolution. It's part of the plan that was designed for you and that you agreed to before you incarnated. No matter what life dumps on you, shake off the dirt, and take a step up.

No one can choose your path for you. Have no regrets about choosing one path over another, thinking that an opportunity was lost. Nothing is ever lost; another opportunity will show up if necessary. Just follow your heart, and trust the magic of new beginnings. Welcome happy surprises, and invite miracles too!

You don't need to be saved and rescued. Be content to be who you are, to be nothing more, nothing less. Remember your own power, and be yourself. Get back to what you loved to do and be as a child, and you will find the real you. There is a force much greater than yourself that you can call upon, so invite this divine wisdom into whatever you find yourself doing. To live in this world requires action. So, take action, and make your dreams happen. The only enemies of your dreams are doubts and fears. When doubts and fears try to take over, remember that these emotions are simply part of the illusion. Do not encourage doubts and fears by giving them attention, and do not resist them. Simply observe them. Something or someone will always appear to help move you forward. Pay attention to the messages, use the tools that you are given, and you will see your map unfold in front of you.

You are exactly where you are supposed to be right now. There's no schedule that you must follow. Your life is exactly on schedule. Live your life in harmony, not fear. You have a choice to be depressed about the past, worried about the future, or being calm in the present. Nothing is real. It's all in your mind.

We're in this game of life together, and we are here for the thrill of the ride, not to fix something that is broken. Let's make it an exhilarating experience!

APPENDIX

Plato's Allegory of the Cave

From Wikipedia, the free encyclopedia - The Allegory of the Cave, or Plato's Cave, was presented by the Greek philosopher Plato in his work Republic (514a–520a). It is written as a dialogue between Plato's brother Glaucon and his mentor Socrates. Socrates describes a group of people who have been chained to the wall of a cave, facing a blank wall, all of their lives. The chained people watch shadows projected on the wall from objects passing in front of a fire behind them, and they give names to these shadows. The shadows are the prisoners' reality. Socrates explains how the philosopher is like a prisoner who is freed from the cave and comes to understand that the shadows on the wall are not reality at all, for he can perceive the true form of reality rather than the manufactured reality that is the shadows seen by the prisoners. The inmates of this place do not even desire to leave their prison; they know no better life. The prisoners manage to break their bonds one day and discover that their reality was not what they thought it was. They discover the sun, which Plato uses as an analogy for the fire that man cannot see behind. Like the fire that casts light on the walls of the cave, the human condition is forever bound to the impressions that are received through the senses. Even if these interpretations are an absurd misrepresentation of reality, we cannot somehow break free from the bonds of our human condition. We cannot free ourselves from a phenomenal state just as the prisoners could not free themselves from their chains. If, however, we were to miraculously escape our bondage, we would find a world that we could not understand. The sun is incomprehensible for someone who has never seen it. In other words, we would encounter another realm, a place incomprehensible because, theoretically, it is the source of a higher reality than the one we have always known.

WORKS CITED

Beckwith, Michael Bernard. https://www.azquotes.com/
quote/839825

Byrne, Rhonda. The Secret. Hillsboro, Oregon: Beyond Words
Publishing, 2006.

Chopra, Deepak. https://www.quotenova.net/authors/
deepak-chopra/q6742e

Coelho, Paulo. https://www.goodreads.com/author/
quotes/16593449.Paul_Coelho

Craig, Gary. The Gary Craig Official EFT. https://www.emofree.
com/english/eft-tapping-tutorial-en.html

Davis, Stephen. Butterflies are Free to Fly: A New and Radical
Approach to Spiritual Evolution. https://www.butterfliesfree.com

Dyer, Dr. Wayne. https://www.drwaynedyer.com/?s=belief

Edgar Cayce's A.R.E. https://www.edgarcayce.org/
search-results/?searchTerm=study+group

Ehrmann, Max. Desiderata. 1927. https://www.desiderata.com/
desiderata.html

Einstein, Albert. https://www.goodreads.com/author/quotes/9810.
Albert_Einstein?page=7

Eliot, T.S. https://www.goodreads.com/quotes/644987-we-shall-not-cease-from-exploration-and-the-end-of

Fortune, Dion. The Mystical Qabalah. San Francisco: Weiser Books, 1935, 1998. Revised edition published 2000.

Gibran, Kahlil. The Prophet. 1923. https://poets.org/poem/children-1

Greene, Brian. "Past, present and future coexist. 'Now time' explained easy." 2017. Video. https://youtu.be/idsw99SSwKc

Grzela, Jocelyne. "Jocelyne with orangutans in Borneo." 2009. Video. https://youtu.be/aFpIfUd1gYA

Grzela, Jocelyne. Simple meditation exercise. 2020. https://jocelynegrzela.com/meditations

Herbert, Nick. https://en.wikiquote.org/wiki/Nick_Herbert_(physicist)

Hicks, Bill. "It's Just a Ride." 1992. Video. https://www.youtube.com/watch?v=KgzQuE1pR1w&feature=youtu.be

Hindu legend. Brahma. http://www.naute.com/stories/hideout.phtml

Holmes, Ernest. https://www.azquotes.com/quote/813444

Maslow, Dr. Abraham. https://www.azquotes.com/quote/481913

Mother Teresa. https://www.azquotes.com/author/14530-Mother_Teresa/tag/war

Murphy, Joseph. The Power of Your Subconscious Mind. Mansfield Centre, Connecticut: Martino Publishing, 2011. Reprint of 1963 Edition.

Nag Hammadi library. Wikipedia. Last edited September 12, 2020. https://en.wikipedia.org/wiki/Nag_Hammadi_library

Pagels, Elaine. The Gnostic Gospels. Vintage, 1989.

Plato. The Cave: An Adaptation of Plato's Allegory in Clay. Denver: Bullhead Entertainment, LLC. 2008. Video. https://youtu.be/69F7GhASOdM

Paffenhoff, Jean-Marie. Les Anges de Votre Vie: Comment leur parler? Paris: France Loisirs, 1995.

Quinn Yarbro, Chelsea. Messages from Michael. London: Penguin Publishing Group, 1995 (first published 1979).

Redfield, James. The Celestine Prophecy. Hoover, Alabama: Satori Publishing, 1993.

Rumi. https://www.azquotes.com/quote/752153

Shakespeare, William. http://www.finestquotes.com/quote-id-4136.htm

Simons, Daniel J. "The Monkey Business Illusion." 2020. Video. https://youtu.be/IGQmdoK_ZfY

Socrates. https://medium.com/@wanha/13-quotes-from-gandhi-to-socrates-to-challenge-your-life-assumptions-d102145d27a6

Swindoll, Charles R. https://www.brainyquote.com/quotes/charles_r_swindoll_388332

Todeshi, Kevin J. The Encyclopedia of Symbolism. New York: Berkley Publishing Group, 1995.

Tolle, Eckhart. https://www.azquotes.com/author/14703-Eckhart_Tolle

Truman, Karol K. Feelings Buried Alive Never Die. St. George, Utah: Olympus Distributing, 1991.

Walsch, Neale Donald. Communion with God: An uncommon dialogue. New York: TarcherPerigee, 2002.

Wolf, Fred Alan, The Dreaming Universe: A Mind-Expanding Journey Into the Realm Where Psyche and Physics Meet. New York: Touchstone, 1995.

* * *

ABOUT THE AUTHOR

Born and raised in a small town in Northern Ontario, Canada, Jocelyne grew up in a loving family of thirteen children, of which she is the youngest.

Though she initially pursued a career as a school teacher, Jocelyne's search for the mysteries of life, the universe, and our place in it, led her on many different paths. She later worked as a radio broadcaster, an office manager, and business owner. Jocelyne moved from Canada to the United States in 1989. She obtained her Hypnotherapist and Past Life Regression Therapist certification from the Association for Research and Enlightenment in Virginia Beach, VA in 2001. She ran a successful practice in Florida from 2001 to 2004, then in Colorado from 2004 to 2005. During this period, she also conducted several workshops on meditation, hypnosis, and reincarnation.

Her desire to make a difference, combined with her entrepreneurial spirit, opened the way for her to co-create a tropical rainforest replanting business in 2005, but following an unexpected series of events, Jocelyne moved back to her native country in 2010. She continues to share her gems of wisdom with those who are put on her path. She lives in Ottawa, Ontario. Visit her at jocelynegrzela.com

Printed in Canada